OLYMPIAD WORKBOOK

INTERNATIONAL ENGLISH OLYMPIAD

AF390165

01 Learning Objectives

02 Multiple Choice Questions

03 HOTS (Achievers Section)

04 Model Test Paper

05 Answer Keys and Solutions

06 OMR Answer Sheet

V&S PUBLISHERS

Published by:

V&S PUBLISHERS

F-2/16, Ansari road, Daryaganj, New Delhi-110002
☎ 23240026, 23240027 • *Fax:* 011-23240028
✉ info@vspublishers.com • ⊕ www.vspublishers.com

Online Brandstore: amazon.in/vspublishers

Regional Office : Hyderabad
5-1-707/1, Brij Bhawan (Beside Central Bank of India Lane)
Bank Street, Koti, Hyderabad - 500 095
☎ 040-24737290
✉ vspublishershyd@gmail.com

Follow us on:   

BUY OUR BOOKS FROM: AMAZON FLIPKART

© Copyright: V&S PUBLISHERS
ISBN 978-81-978021-5-7
New Edition

DISCLAIMER

While every attempt has been made to provide accurate and timely information in this book, neither the author nor the publisher assumes any responsibility for errors, unintended omissions or commissions detected therein. The author and publisher makes no representation or warranty with respect to the comprehensiveness or completeness of the contents provided.

All matters included have been simplified under professional guidance for general information only, without any warranty for applicability on an individual. Any mention of an organization or a website in the book, by way of citation or as a source of additional information, doesn't imply the endorsement of the content either by the author or the publisher. It is possible that websites cited may have changed or removed between the time of editing and publishing the book.

Results from using the expert opinion in this book will be totally dependent on individual circumstances and factors beyond the control of the author and the publisher.

It makes sense to elicit advice from well informed sources before implementing the ideas given in the book. The reader assumes full responsibility for the consequences arising out from reading this book.

For proper guidance, it is advisable to read the book under the watchful eyes of parents/guardian. The buyer of this book assumes all responsibility for the use of given materials and information.

The copyright of the entire content of this book rests with the author/publisher. Any infringement/transmission of the cover design, text or illustrations, in any form, by any means, by any entity will invite legal action and be responsible for consequences thereon.

PUBLISHER'S NOTE

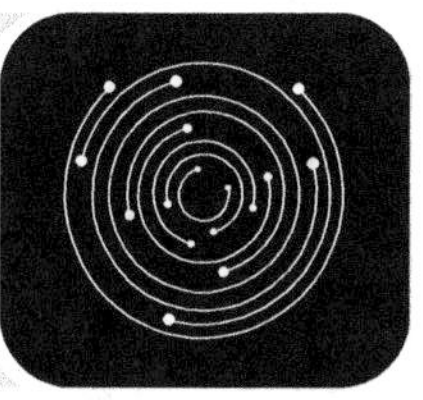

V&S Publishers has carved a significant niche in the publishing industry over the last decade, having successfully published more than 1000 titles across 9 languages spanning over 50 subject categories. Being known for the quality of content, we have built a reputation of excellence and reliability. We have consistently delivered **"Value & Substance"** to our readers, through a wide range of titles across a variety of genres covering school books, fiction and non-fiction that caters to different people from every section of the society.

The **Olympiad Guidebooks for classes 1-10** across all subjects, launched almost a decade ago, under the **GEN X Imprint**, became a go-to-source for the school students in no time, owing to their invaluable and substantive content written in a guidebook pattern,.

Having successfully sold a million copies of the same and in response to demand by both students as well as shopkeepers nationwide; we now present before you our newly launched **Olympiad Workbook Series**, designed for **classes 1-10 across 4 subjects**.

The workbooks are meticulously curated by a team of experienced educators, researchers and subject matter experts, edited by professionals and peer reviewed by teachers. The team has poured its efforts and expertise into creating a crisp and concise workbook which will help and guide the students to the path of success in Olympiad exams. The **MCQs** identified will not only help in scoring top marks in Olympiads but also inculcate a sense of deeper understanding of the subject, by way of solving **HOTS** and referring to complete solutions at the end of the book.

Here we present our new release– **OLYMPIAD WORKBOOK (IEO) CLASS–5** having following features:

- Based on the latest syllabi
- MCQs with comprehensive coverage of topics
- HOTS Questions liberally included
- A dedicated chapter on logical reasoning
- Model test paper for thorough practice
- Sample OMR sheet for real time simulation

We have made sure through our best efforts, that this workbook strictly follows the latest syllabi and patterns of the Olympiad Examination.

As **V&S Publishers** continuously strive to enhance the readability and maintain the credibility of our academic publications, we seek the support of our valuable readers in influencing and enriching the lives of future generations of students.

P.S. While every care has been taken to ensure the correctness of the content, if you come across any error, howsoever minor, do not hesitate to discuss with teachers while pointing that out to us in no uncertain terms.

We wish you all the best for your exams!

DISTINCTIVE FEATURES

01

Learning Objectives

They list the whole chapter as subtopics, helping the teachers to guide children in a step-by-step manner.

02

Multiple Choice Questions

MCQs act as an excellent learning aid, helping you to understand and work on your mistakes.

03

HOTS (Achievers Section)

The High Order Thinking Questions aim to help the student to solve Application-based questions and gain practical understanding of the subject.

04

Model Test Paper

Model test paper are provided at the end of each book, which help the student to test the knowledge which they have gained after thorough reading of all chapters.

05

Answer Key

Detailed Answer Key along with explanations aid the pupil to indentify, understand the mistakes they make during the course of Olympiad preparation.

CONTENTS

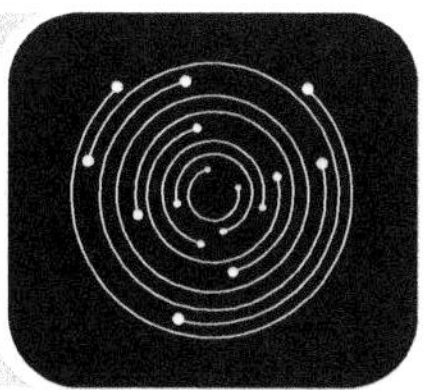

WORD POWER

LEARNING OBJECTIVES

➤ In this chapter, students will learn about:
➤ General Categories of Food
➤ Character

PRACTICE EXERCISE

I. Which of the options is not a synonym for the emotion mentioned here?

1. Anger
   (A) Fury (B) Rage
   (C) Violence (D) Joy

2. Disgust
   (A) Loathing (B) Revulsion
   (C) Approval (D) Antipathy

3. Surprise
   (A) Mundane (B) Revelation
   (C) Bewilderment (D) Amazement

4. Calm
   (A) Tranquil (B) Nervous
   (C) Harmonious (D) Cool

5. Dejected
   (A) Discouraged (B) Gloomy
   (C) Heartened (D) Morose

6. Awed
   (A) Admiration (B) Expectation
   (C) Wonder (D) Astonishment

7. Hurt
   (A) Agony (B) Injury
   (C) Ease (D) Torment

8. Surprised
   (A) Amazed (B) Startled
   (C) Taken aback (D) Poised

9. Sleepy
   (A) Alert (B) Drowsy
   (C) Lethargic (D) Sluggish

10. Confused
   (A) Baffled (B) Composed
   (C) Perplexed (D) Puzzled11.

II. What mode of transportation is used in each of these sentences? (train, flight, road or boat/ship)

11. Dad drove us to Jaipur in our car.

12. It took us 3 hours in an aeroplane to reach Chennai.

13. Due to bad weather, our plane journey was uncomfortable.

14. The fastest trains in India are Raj-dhani and Shatabdi.

15. India has two heritage hill railways.

16. The bus service to Shimla is very good.

17. India has the largest network of railways in the world.

18. Due to fog, planes were delayed by many hours.

19. One can go to Andaman Islands by sea route as well.
20. There are many small islands in the pacific ocean where there are no airports.

III. Provide a synonym of the underlined word.

21. She is an extremely <u>unfriendly</u> person.
22. The driver's <u>negligence</u> was the cause of the accident.
23. Neha got a <u>fair</u> deal on her bike.
24. Rahul Dravid was regarded as an extremely <u>dependable</u> player.
25. A soldier's <u>courage</u> is comparable to that of a lion.

HOTS (ACHIEVERS SECTION)

26. Mood is defined as
   (A) A short-lived feeling
   (B) Being depressed for more than 1 month
   (C) A prevailing state of feeling
   (D) A temporary depression

26. When speakers are having a difficult day "keeping it together", they would use which of the following words to describe this experience?
   (A) Fear   (B) Anxiety
   (C) Angst   (D) Sadness

28. Which is called body building foods?
   (A) Proteins   (B) Fats
   (C) Carbohydrates (D) all of these

29. Foods have various __________ that keep us healthy.
   (A) nutrients   (B) all of these
   (C) components   (D) substances

30. Feeling of tiredness, weight loss, excessive thirst are symptoms of
   (A) Marasmus   (B) Dengue
   (C) Diabetese   (D) Obesity

SYNONYMS AND ANTONYMS

LEARNING OBJECTIVES

➤ Synonyms
➤ Antonyms

PRACTICE EXERCISE

Direction: In each of the following groups, one word is followed by four words or expressions. One of the four words or expressions is the synonym of this wor(D)

1. Pick up the synonym.
   Fable
   (A) truth   (B) dirt
   (C) myth   (D) sanity

2. Pick up the synonym.
   Let
   (A) silence   (B) speech
   (C) permit   (D) dexterity

3. Pick up the synonym.
   Knave
   (A) facility   (B) difficulty
   (C) hardness   (D) rogue

4. Pick up the synonym.
   Mode
   (A) veracity   (B) dishonesty
   (C) method   (D) debate

5. Pick up the synonym.
   Waspish
   (A) fishy   (B) i3eevisb
   (C) amiable   (D) heroic

6. Pick up the synonym.
   Brilliant
   (A) hearty   (B) bold
   (C) splendid   (D) sly

7. Pick up the synonym.
   Prudent
   (A) puny   (B) burly
   (C) cautious   (D) indecent

8. Pick up the synonym.
   Meet
   (A) truthful   (B) nimble
   (C) suitable   (D) unfit

9. Pick up the synonym.
   Better
   (A) batter   (B) vaunt
   (C) deject   (D) improve

10. Pick up the synonym.
    Court
    (A) shun   (B) fade
    (C) cavil   (D) tribunal

11. Pick up the synonym.
    Face
    (A) allay   (B) falter
    (C) confront   (D) foment

12. Pick up the synonym.
Kid
(A) assist   (B) revive
(C) prolong   (D) young one

13. Pick up the synonym.
Lessen
(A) expand   (B) wilt
(C) decrease   (D) Elapse

14. Pick up the synonym.
Needled
(A) please   (B) amass
(C) annoy   (D) gladden

15. Pick up the synonym.
Quest
(A) hide   (B) agitate
(C) request   (D) Search

16. Pick up the synonym.
Rag
(A) Raid   (B) rub
(C) falsify   (D) tease

17. Pick up the synonym.
Tail
(A) snub
(B) match
(C) distend
(D) follow somebody closed

18. Pick up the synonym.
Refresh
(A) enjoy   (B) regroup
(C) renew   (D) weary

19. Pick up the synonym.
Slight
(A) minor   (B) flatter
(C) quibble   (D) comfort

20. Pick up the synonym.
Yield
(A) fend
(B) found

(C) flout
(D) concede

21. Pick up the synonym.
Slam
(A) help
(B) loss
(C) request
(D) smash

Direction: In each of the following groups, one word is followed by four words or expressions.

22. Pick up the word or expression having the opposite meaning of this word:
Summit
(A) peak
(B) vertex
(C) foundation
(D) nadir

23. Pick up the word or expression having the opposite meaning of this word:
Loyalty
(A) disloyalty
(B) disbelief
(C) sermon
(D) slut

24. Pick up the word or expression having the opposite meaning of this word:
Dishonesty
(A) indecency
(B) rudeness
(C) impropriety
(D) probity

25. Pick up the word or expression having the opposite meaning of this word:
Hazard
(A) peril
(B) risk
(C) excursion
(D) safety

Direction: In each of the following groups, one word is followed by four words or expressions. One of the four words or expressions is the synonym of this wor(D)

26. Pick up the synonym.

    Dilemma

    (A) vigour   (B) force

    (C) delight   (D) predicament

27. Pick up the synonym.

    Knack

    (A) rogue   (B) peril

    (C) safety   (D) bent

28. Pick up the synonym.

    Foe

    (A) fool   (B) fealty

    (C) logic   (D) enemy

Direction: In each of the following groups, one word is followed by four words or expressions.

29. Pick up the word or expression having the opposite meaning of this word:

    Ability

    (A) competence   (B) esteem

    (C) hare   (D) inability

30. Pick up the word or expression having the opposite meaning of this word:

    Alliance

    (A) adversary   (B) friendship

    (C) concord   (D) combination

—Darken Your Choice with HB Pencil—

1.	Ⓐ Ⓑ Ⓒ Ⓓ	7.	Ⓐ Ⓑ Ⓒ Ⓓ	13.	Ⓐ Ⓑ Ⓒ Ⓓ	19	Ⓐ Ⓑ Ⓒ Ⓓ	25.	Ⓐ Ⓑ Ⓒ Ⓓ
2.	Ⓐ Ⓑ Ⓒ Ⓓ	8.	Ⓐ Ⓑ Ⓒ Ⓓ	14.	Ⓐ Ⓑ Ⓒ Ⓓ	20.	Ⓐ Ⓑ Ⓒ Ⓓ	26.	Ⓐ Ⓑ Ⓒ Ⓓ
3.	Ⓐ Ⓑ Ⓒ Ⓓ	9.	Ⓐ Ⓑ Ⓒ Ⓓ	15.	Ⓐ Ⓑ Ⓒ Ⓓ	21.	Ⓐ Ⓑ Ⓒ Ⓓ	27.	Ⓐ Ⓑ Ⓒ Ⓓ
4.	Ⓐ Ⓑ Ⓒ Ⓓ	10.	Ⓐ Ⓑ Ⓒ Ⓓ	16.	Ⓐ Ⓑ Ⓒ Ⓓ	22.	Ⓐ Ⓑ Ⓒ Ⓓ	28.	Ⓐ Ⓑ Ⓒ Ⓓ
5.	Ⓐ Ⓑ Ⓒ Ⓓ	11.	Ⓐ Ⓑ Ⓒ Ⓓ	17.	Ⓐ Ⓑ Ⓒ Ⓓ	23.	Ⓐ Ⓑ Ⓒ Ⓓ	29.	Ⓐ Ⓑ Ⓒ Ⓓ
6.	Ⓐ Ⓑ Ⓒ Ⓓ	12.	Ⓐ Ⓑ Ⓒ Ⓓ	18.	Ⓐ Ⓑ Ⓒ Ⓓ	24.	Ⓐ Ⓑ Ⓒ Ⓓ	30.	Ⓐ Ⓑ Ⓒ Ⓓ

HOMONYMS AND HOMOPHONES

3

LEARNING OBJECTIVES

➤ Homonyms and Homophones

PRACTICE EXERCISE

I. Choose the correct word from similar sounding words given below

1. The doctor's ___ waited outside the office.
   (A) patience   (B) patients

2. A drink of water will clear the ___.
   (A) palate   (B) palette

3. One can easily get lost in a ___.
   (A) maize   (B) maze

4. Set another ___ at the table because we are expecting a guest.
   (A) place   (B) plaice

5. The ___ filled with water until it burst.
   (A) hoes   (B) hose

6. How can you make such a ___ suggestion?
   (A) vial   (B) vile

7. Not all poetry has a ___ scheme.
   (A) rhyme   (B) rime

8. She dresses with style and ___.
   (A) flair   (B) flare

9. In an emergency use a ___ to attract attention.
   (A) flair   (B) flare

10. We use ___ to loosen the soil and cut away weeds.
    (A) hoes   (B) hose

11. I want to ___ you for your beautiful painting.
    (A) complement   (B) compliment

12. The ___ rushed in and covered the beach.
    (A) tide   (B) tied

13. The ___ bear is a very dangerous animal.
    (A) grisly   (B) grizzly

14. Grandfather was a ___ and hearty man.
    (A) hail   (B) hale

15. What have you ___ that is so frightening?
    (A) scene   (B) seen

16. Tell me directly. Don't just ___ to some problem.
    (A) elude   (B) allude

17. He squeezed out a ___ of power at the end of the race.
    (A) serge   (B) surge

18. There is a ___ in my eye.
    (A) moat   (B) mote

19. She likes to ride the roller coaster for the ___ thrill of it.
    (A) shear   (B) sheer

20. A small sample is over there in the glass ___.
    (A) file   (B) phial

II. Fill in the blanks.

21. By the time we reached, __________, the shop was already closed. (there/their)

22. Are you going ____________ see the circus ____________? (to/too/two)

23. I will __________ the essay today. (right/write)

24. Neha ________ the ____________ cake by herself. (eight/ate; hole/whole)

25. The glass ____________ broke on being hit by the stone. (pain/pane)

HOTS (ACHIEVERS SECTION)

I. Fill in the blanks with the correct option.

26. He skidded because he did not apply the ________.

(A) break   (B) brakes
(C) both   (D) neither

27. You should not lose ______ in this situation.

(A) hurt   (B) hart
(C) heart   (D) hard

28. What is the ______ of this shirt?

(A) price   (B) prize
(C) preys   (D) cast

29. We ______ the potato with a knife.

(A) peal   (B) open
(C) heel   (D) peel

30. Every airport has a __________.

(A) hunger
(B) hanger
(C) hangar
(D) none of the above

Darken Your Choice with HB Pencil

1. Ⓐ Ⓑ Ⓒ Ⓓ	7. Ⓐ Ⓑ Ⓒ Ⓓ	13. Ⓐ Ⓑ Ⓒ Ⓓ	19 Ⓐ Ⓑ Ⓒ Ⓓ	25. Ⓐ Ⓑ Ⓒ Ⓓ
2. Ⓐ Ⓑ Ⓒ Ⓓ	8. Ⓐ Ⓑ Ⓒ Ⓓ	14. Ⓐ Ⓑ Ⓒ Ⓓ	20. Ⓐ Ⓑ Ⓒ Ⓓ	26. Ⓐ Ⓑ Ⓒ Ⓓ
3. Ⓐ Ⓑ Ⓒ Ⓓ	9. Ⓐ Ⓑ Ⓒ Ⓓ	15. Ⓐ Ⓑ Ⓒ Ⓓ	21. Ⓐ Ⓑ Ⓒ Ⓓ	27. Ⓐ Ⓑ Ⓒ Ⓓ
4. Ⓐ Ⓑ Ⓒ Ⓓ	10. Ⓐ Ⓑ Ⓒ Ⓓ	16. Ⓐ Ⓑ Ⓒ Ⓓ	22. Ⓐ Ⓑ Ⓒ Ⓓ	28. Ⓐ Ⓑ Ⓒ Ⓓ
5. Ⓐ Ⓑ Ⓒ Ⓓ	11. Ⓐ Ⓑ Ⓒ Ⓓ	17. Ⓐ Ⓑ Ⓒ Ⓓ	23. Ⓐ Ⓑ Ⓒ Ⓓ	29. Ⓐ Ⓑ Ⓒ Ⓓ
6. Ⓐ Ⓑ Ⓒ Ⓓ	12. Ⓐ Ⓑ Ⓒ Ⓓ	18. Ⓐ Ⓑ Ⓒ Ⓓ	24. Ⓐ Ⓑ Ⓒ Ⓓ	30. Ⓐ Ⓑ Ⓒ Ⓓ

COLLOCATION AND IDIOMS

LEARNING OBJECTIVES

➤ Types of Collocations
➤ Idiom

PRACTICE EXERCISE

I. Choose the correct options that explains the meaning of the idioms.

1. To end in smoke
    (A) Smoking too many cigarettes
    (B) House burnt down
    (C) Face failure
    (D) Religious ceremony

2. To get into hot waters
    (A) Bathe in the winter months
    (B) To get healthy
    (C) To get rich
    (D) To get into trouble

3. To make ends meet
    (A) A short story
    (B) To earn enough to live
    (C) To skip classes
    (D) To be an expert

4. Bolt from the blue
    (A) Sudden shock
    (B) To get punched
    (C) To lose a tight game
    (D) To ask for help

5. To burn the candle at both ends
    (A) To argue endlessly
    (B) Long power cut
    (C) To work long hours
    (D) To have a good time

6. To bury the hatchet
    (A) To end enmity
    (B) To kill someone
    (C) To hide stolen treasure
    (D) To overexert

7. To spill the beans
    (A) To eat clumsily
    (B) To reveal a secret
    (C) To get exhausted
    (D) To fight

8. To lead someone up the garden path
    (A) To give directions
    (B) To show a beautiful place
    (C) To mislead someone
    (D) To exaggerate

9. To weather a storm
    (A) To criticize someone
    (B) To survive a crisis
    (C) To be an introvert
    (D) To guess correctly

10. To bite one's tongue
    (A) To be unsure
    (B) To feel sorry at someone's plight
    (C) To not react despite being angry
    (D) To laugh at someone's misfortune

II. Complete the idiom with the correct word to make meaningful sentences

11. He is all ________ and can't install or repair anything in the house.
    (A) elbows   (B) knees
    (C) thumbs   (D) toes

12. She decided to try her __________ at gardening.
    (A) body   (B) hand
    (C) head   (D) leg

13. She didn't have the ____________ to tell him the bad news.
    (A) heart   (B) mouth
    (C) soul   (D) tongue

14. It will be difficult for him to save ________ after such a terrible blunder.
    (A) body   (B) face
    (C) hair   (D) head

15. She has a good ________ for music.
    (A) ear   (B) eye
    (C) finger   (D) nose

16. Her flower garden is fantastic She loves gardening and has a ________ thumb.
    (A) blue   (B) green
    (C) red   (D) white

17. The idea came to him right out of the ________ when he was making coffee in the kitchen.
    (A) blue   (B) green
    (C) red   (D) white

18. There was so much bureaucratic ________ tapism that we did not get the required papers in time.
    (A) blue   (B) green
    (C) red   (D) white

19. He is the ________ sheep of the family.
    (A) black   (B) gray
    (C) pink   (D) purple

20. Every cloud has a ________ lining.
    (A) black   (B) golden
    (C) gray   (D) silver

III. Choose the correct option to complete the collocation

21. He spoke English with a ____ French accent.
    (A) average   (B) careless
    (C) widespread   (D) pronounced

22. He gave us a ________ account of all that you had achieved over there.
    (A) ready   (B) yellow
    (C) careless   (D) glowing

23. He was able to predict what was going to happen with ________ accuracy.
    (A) itemised   (B) uncanny
    (C) careless   (D) glowing

24. They've made some highly ________ accusations about us.
    (A) itemised   (B) uncanny
    (C) damaging   (D) luxury

25. This will probably be the ____________ achievement of her career.
    (A) itemised   (B) uncanny
    (C) damaging   (D) crowning

I. Select the correct meaning of the underlined word from the options given.

26. It's raining cats and dogs today. We will have to cancel our field trip.
    - (A) It's sunny
    - (B) Cats and dogs are playing in the rain
    - (C) It's raining heavily
    - (D) It's very warm

27. Samuel lost the project file. It meant we had to start the project from scratch.
    - (A) Cancel
    - (B) Finish
    - (C) Find
    - (D) Beginning

28. Amanda thanked Derek from the bottom of her heart for helping her.
    - (A) Unfriendly
    - (B) Falsely
    - (C) Angrily
    - (D) Sincerely

29. Everyone in the town knows that Mr. Mathew has a heart of gold.
    - (A) Mr. Mathew is a selfish.
    - (B) Mr. Mathew has lots of gold.
    - (C) Mr. Mathew is a very kind and honest person.
    - (D) Mr. Mathew has a heart problem.

30. When Julia won the Best Student of the Year Award, Kristy was green with envy.
    - (A) Kristy was happy
    - (B) Kristy was jealous
    - (C) Kristy painted her face green
    - (D) Kristy fell sick

Darken Your Choice with HB Pencil

1.	Ⓐ Ⓑ Ⓒ Ⓓ	7.	Ⓐ Ⓑ Ⓒ Ⓓ	13.	Ⓐ Ⓑ Ⓒ Ⓓ	19	Ⓐ Ⓑ Ⓒ Ⓓ	25.	Ⓐ Ⓑ Ⓒ Ⓓ
2.	Ⓐ Ⓑ Ⓒ Ⓓ	8.	Ⓐ Ⓑ Ⓒ Ⓓ	14.	Ⓐ Ⓑ Ⓒ Ⓓ	20.	Ⓐ Ⓑ Ⓒ Ⓓ	26.	Ⓐ Ⓑ Ⓒ Ⓓ
3.	Ⓐ Ⓑ Ⓒ Ⓓ	9.	Ⓐ Ⓑ Ⓒ Ⓓ	15.	Ⓐ Ⓑ Ⓒ Ⓓ	21.	Ⓐ Ⓑ Ⓒ Ⓓ	27.	Ⓐ Ⓑ Ⓒ Ⓓ
4.	Ⓐ Ⓑ Ⓒ Ⓓ	10.	Ⓐ Ⓑ Ⓒ Ⓓ	16.	Ⓐ Ⓑ Ⓒ Ⓓ	22.	Ⓐ Ⓑ Ⓒ Ⓓ	28.	Ⓐ Ⓑ Ⓒ Ⓓ
5.	Ⓐ Ⓑ Ⓒ Ⓓ	11.	Ⓐ Ⓑ Ⓒ Ⓓ	17.	Ⓐ Ⓑ Ⓒ Ⓓ	23.	Ⓐ Ⓑ Ⓒ Ⓓ	29.	Ⓐ Ⓑ Ⓒ Ⓓ
6.	Ⓐ Ⓑ Ⓒ Ⓓ	12.	Ⓐ Ⓑ Ⓒ Ⓓ	18.	Ⓐ Ⓑ Ⓒ Ⓓ	24.	Ⓐ Ⓑ Ⓒ Ⓓ	30.	Ⓐ Ⓑ Ⓒ Ⓓ

NOUN

LEARNING OBJECTIVES

➤ Types of Noun
➤ Uses of Noun

PRACTICE EXERCISE

I. Choose the correct noun from the alternatives and fill in the blanks given in every sentence:

1. The radio is a wonderful source of _______
   (A) inform   (B) informative
   (C) informatively   (D) information

2. Your passport shows your _______
   (A) nation   (B) national
   (C) nationality   (D) nationalist

3. What forms of _______ do you like?
   (A) entertains   (B) entertain
   (C) entertainment   (D) entertainingly

4. A person of his _______ will get a job easily.
   (A) able   (B) unable
   (C) ability   (D) valour

5. You can show your voter ID to show your _______.
   (A) identify
   (B) identifiable
   (C) identified
   (D) identity

6. We need a _______ to help us understand this letter. It's written in French.
   (A) translate   (B) translating
   (C) translated   (D) translator

7. The Indian warriors showed exceptional _______.
   (A) brave   (B) braving
   (C) braved   (D) bravery

8. How did the universe come into _______?
   (A) exist   (B) existence
   (C) existing   (D) existed

9. The United Nations is an inter-national _______.
   (A) organize   (B) organization
   (C) organizer   (D) organized

10. We saw a ____ of sheep on our way to school.
    (A) fleet   (B) flight
    (C) flock   (D) colony

11. Police have arrested a ____ of miscreants.
    (A) group   (B) gathering
    (C) gang   (D) crowd

12. She bought a _______ of bananas from the market.
    (A) cluster   (B) bunch
    (C) group   (D) number

13. You can put the _______ of tools in that box.
    (A) box   (B) set
    (C) group   (D) number

14. There are _____ fishes in the pond.
   (A) much
   (B) a large number of
   (C) few
   (D) a

15. Yesterday I lost my _____ of keys.
   (A) bouquet
   (B) bunch
   (C) bundle
   (D) packet

HOTS (ACHIEVERS SECTION)

Choose the correct noun from the alternatives and fill in the blanks given in every sentence:

16. The radio is a wonderful source of _____
   (A) inform   (B) informative
   (C) informatively   (D) information

17. Your passport shows your _____
   (A) nation   (B) national
   (C) nationality   (D) nationalist

18. What forms of _____ do you like?
   (A) entertains   (B) entertain
   (C) entertainment   (D) entertainingly

19. A person of his _____ will get a job easily.
   (A) able
   (B) unable
   (C) ability
   (D) valour

20. You can show your voter ID to show your _____.
   (A) identify
   (B) identifiable
   (C) identified
   (D) identity

	A B C D		A B C D		A B C D		A B C D		A B C D
1.	Ⓐ Ⓑ Ⓒ Ⓓ	5.	Ⓐ Ⓑ Ⓒ Ⓓ	9.	Ⓐ Ⓑ Ⓒ Ⓓ	13	Ⓐ Ⓑ Ⓒ Ⓓ	17.	Ⓐ Ⓑ Ⓒ Ⓓ
2.	Ⓐ Ⓑ Ⓒ Ⓓ	6.	Ⓐ Ⓑ Ⓒ Ⓓ	10.	Ⓐ Ⓑ Ⓒ Ⓓ	14.	Ⓐ Ⓑ Ⓒ Ⓓ	18.	Ⓐ Ⓑ Ⓒ Ⓓ
3.	Ⓐ Ⓑ Ⓒ Ⓓ	7.	Ⓐ Ⓑ Ⓒ Ⓓ	11.	Ⓐ Ⓑ Ⓒ Ⓓ	15.	Ⓐ Ⓑ Ⓒ Ⓓ	19.	Ⓐ Ⓑ Ⓒ Ⓓ
4.	Ⓐ Ⓑ Ⓒ Ⓓ	8.	Ⓐ Ⓑ Ⓒ Ⓓ	12.	Ⓐ Ⓑ Ⓒ Ⓓ	16.	Ⓐ Ⓑ Ⓒ Ⓓ	20.	Ⓐ Ⓑ Ⓒ Ⓓ

PRONOUN

LEARNING OBJECTIVES

➤ Kinds of Pronoun

PRACTICE EXERCISE

I. Fill in the blanks with appropriate Personal Pronoun given in the options.

1. Her name is Sneha, and _________ is from Dehradun.
   (A) It   (B) She
   (C) You   (D) They

2. His dog has got a long tail. ____________ is dark brown.
   (A) They   (B) You
   (C) We   (D) It

3. Rahul is very tall. ____________ is slim too.
   (A) You   (B) He
   (C) I   (D) She

4. My parents are going to Kerala. __________ are coming back soon.
   (A) It   (B) She
   (C) You   (D) They

5. My name is Richa. ____________ am from Bihar.
   (A) I   (B) He
   (C) It   (D) You

6. Mona and I are sisters. ___________ are from Garhwal region.
   (A) She   (B) They
   (C) You   (D) We

7. Kasturee and you speak English fluently. Where did ____________ learn it from?
   (A) You   (B) They
   (C) I   (D) She

8. Sonam is a good student. _______ always completes her homework.
   (A) I   (B) He
   (C) It   (D) She

9. Mom told ____________ and my sister to never accept sweets from strangers.
   (A) I   (B) Me
   (C) Us   (D) He

10. ___________ went to Nainital in summer vacations.
    (A) It   (B) His
    (C) We   (D) You

II. Fill in the blanks with appropriate Relative Pronoun given in the brackets.

11. Nikhil and Shikha, ________ (that /who) got married about a year ago, recently bought a new house.

12. The neighbourhood ___________ (that/ in which) they have been living in is somewhat a dangerous one.

13. And, the neighbourhood ________ (that / who) they are moving into is not much safer.

14. Shagun's new house, ___________ (that / which) she bought quite cheaply, needs some fixing up.

15. Jake, _______________ (whom / whose) company is nearby, will be able to walk to work.

16. What's the name of the man ______ (whom/whose) car you borrowed?

17. A cemetery is a place ___________ (whom/where) people are buried.

18. The place _______________ (where/who) we spent our holidays was really beautiful.

19. This school is only for children ________________(whose/who) first language is not English.

20. I don't know the name of the woman to ______________ (whom/whose) I spoke on the phone.

III. Fill in the blanks with appropriate Pronoun given in the options.

21. The old woman lived alone, with ___________to look after ___________.
    (A) someone, her
    (B) anyone, herself
    (C) everyone, she
    (D) no one, her
    (E) anyone, she's

22. _________ two rings here on my little finger belonged to _________ grandmother.
    (A) These, my
    (B) That, mine
    (C) Those, me
    (D) The, myself
    (E) This, my

23. When the little boy grabbed the lizard, _________ tail broke off in _________ hand.
    (A) it's, his
    (B) it, him
    (C) its, his
    (D) it, one's
    (E) its, he's

24. A baby learns the meaning of words as ___________ are spoken by others and later uses ___________ in sentences.
    (A) their, they   (B) they, them
    (C) they, themselves (D) it, them
    (E) they, it

25. Some of these clothes are ________and the rest of ___________ belong to Richa.
    (A) yours, it
    (B) my, them
    (C) hers, their
    (D) me, they
    (E) mine, them

Complete the table of pronouns:

Subject Pronoun	Object Pronoun	Possessive Pronoun	Reflexive pronoun
26. they	them	–	themselves
27. she	–	hers	–
28. –	–	–	–
29. you	–	–	–
30. we	–	–	–

Darken Your Choice with HB Pencil

1. Ⓐ Ⓑ Ⓒ Ⓓ	7. Ⓐ Ⓑ Ⓒ Ⓓ	13. Ⓐ Ⓑ Ⓒ Ⓓ	19 Ⓐ Ⓑ Ⓒ Ⓓ	25. Ⓐ Ⓑ Ⓒ Ⓓ
2. Ⓐ Ⓑ Ⓒ Ⓓ	8. Ⓐ Ⓑ Ⓒ Ⓓ	14. Ⓐ Ⓑ Ⓒ Ⓓ	20. Ⓐ Ⓑ Ⓒ Ⓓ	26. Ⓐ Ⓑ Ⓒ Ⓓ
3. Ⓐ Ⓑ Ⓒ Ⓓ	9. Ⓐ Ⓑ Ⓒ Ⓓ	15. Ⓐ Ⓑ Ⓒ Ⓓ	21. Ⓐ Ⓑ Ⓒ Ⓓ	27. Ⓐ Ⓑ Ⓒ Ⓓ
4. Ⓐ Ⓑ Ⓒ Ⓓ	10. Ⓐ Ⓑ Ⓒ Ⓓ	16. Ⓐ Ⓑ Ⓒ Ⓓ	22. Ⓐ Ⓑ Ⓒ Ⓓ	28. Ⓐ Ⓑ Ⓒ Ⓓ
5. Ⓐ Ⓑ Ⓒ Ⓓ	11. Ⓐ Ⓑ Ⓒ Ⓓ	17. Ⓐ Ⓑ Ⓒ Ⓓ	23. Ⓐ Ⓑ Ⓒ Ⓓ	29. Ⓐ Ⓑ Ⓒ Ⓓ
6. Ⓐ Ⓑ Ⓒ Ⓓ	12. Ⓐ Ⓑ Ⓒ Ⓓ	18. Ⓐ Ⓑ Ⓒ Ⓓ	24. Ⓐ Ⓑ Ⓒ Ⓓ	30. Ⓐ Ⓑ Ⓒ Ⓓ

VERBS AND ADVERBS

LEARNING OBJECTIVES

➤ Basic concept of Verbs and Adverbs
➤ Types of Verbs

PRACTICE EXERCISE

I. Complete each sentence correctly by filling in the blanks with correct form of the verb given in brackets

1. No one answered when the milkman ________________ (ring) the doorbell.

2. Last Sunday morning we discovered that the tank in our building had ____________(spring) a leak.

3. Priya went to the blackboard and ____________(draw) a picture of the playground.

4. Don't call the world dirty because you ______________ (forget) to clean your glasses.

5. Shikha had never ____________ (ride) in a roller coaster before.

6. When we were five years old, Mohit and I solemnly ______________ (swear) to remain friends forever.

7. Meera had ______________ (mean) to send her father a birthday card, but as usual she forgot.

8. My uncle had ______________ (go) to the post office at lunch time but never came back.

9. Trying to be good Samaritans had ______________ (bring) us nothing but trouble.

10. The student insisted that someone had ______________ (steal) his sunglasses, but everyone could see that they were still sitting on top of his head.

II. In each sentence replace the verb in bold with the correct phrasal verb/ choice given in the options.

11. Quick! **Board** the bus. It's ready to leave.
    (A) Get for
    (B) Get on
    (C) Look down
    (D) Put on

12. I don't know where my book is. I have to **search** it.
    (A) Look for
    (B) Look in
    (C) Look out
    (D) Look down

13. It's dark inside. Can you turn on the light, please?
    (A) Switch away
    (B) Take on

(C) Look out
(D) Switch on

14. Complete the form, please.
   (A) Fill up
   (B) Fill in
   (C) Get on
   (D) Turn in

15. Would you like to check out these jeans?
   (A) Try up
   (B) Try in
   (C) Try on
   (D) Try of

III. Choose the correct adverb from the options given below and fill in the blanks:

16. We are standing __________ his house waiting for him.
   (A) outside
   (B) yesterday
   (C) never
   (D) angrily

17. He told us _____ not to walk on the grass.
   (A) outside
   (B) yesterday
   (C) never
   (D) angrily

18. I am not strong ________ to help him carry that box.
   (A) enough
   (B) yesterday
   (C) never
   (D) angrily

19. She will ________ be happy in that job.
   (A) enough
   (B) yesterday

(C) never
(D) angrily

20. My father is ________ late for work.
   (A) quickly
   (B) rarely
   (C) down
   (D) last week

21. He drove ________ to avoid being late.
   (A) down
   (B) quickly
   (C) rarely
   (D) often

22. I ______ play badminton with my sister.
   (A) rarely
   (B) quickly
   (C) often
   (D) down

23. They were __________ very friendly.
   (A) just
   (B) nearly
   (C) always
   (D) online

24. She has ________ completed her degree course.
   (A) just
   (B) nearly
   (C) unusually
   (D) online

25. Shivani is happy. She smiles ________.
   (A) happier
   (B) happiest
   (C) happily
   (D) happy

I. Change these verbs to their irregular forms.

26. swim → ________ → ________

27. write → ________ → ________

1. Read the statements and choose true or false.

Statement A: Adverbs are words that modify nouns and pronouns.

Statement B: Adjectives are words that modify verbs, adverbs and other adjectives.

(A) Only A is true.

(B) Only B is true.

(C) Both A and B are true.

(D) Both A and B are false.

28. Read the statements and choose true or false.

Statement A: Both adverbs and adjectives modify each other.

Statement B: Adverbs take the place of verbs in some instances.

(A) Only A is true.

(B) Only B is true.

(C) Both A and B are true.

(D) Both A and Bare false.

29. Select the sentence in which "usually" appears in an appropriate position.

(A) She usually shops for clothes at the local thrift store.

(B) Usually she shops for clothes at the local thrift store.

(C) She shops for clothes at the local thrift store usually.

(D) Either "A" or "B" is fine.

30. Identify the kind of a Verb (Time, Frequency, Place, Manner): Unlike other summers, we will seldom go out because mom will soon give birth to my baby brother.

(A) Time

(B) Frequency

(C) Place

(D) Manner

	A	B	C	D		A	B	C	D		A	B	C	D		A	B	C	D		A	B	C	D
1.	Ⓐ	Ⓑ	Ⓒ	Ⓓ	7.	Ⓐ	Ⓑ	Ⓒ	Ⓓ	13.	Ⓐ	Ⓑ	Ⓒ	Ⓓ	19	Ⓐ	Ⓑ	Ⓒ	Ⓓ	25.	Ⓐ	Ⓑ	Ⓒ	Ⓓ
2.	Ⓐ	Ⓑ	Ⓒ	Ⓓ	8.	Ⓐ	Ⓑ	Ⓒ	Ⓓ	14.	Ⓐ	Ⓑ	Ⓒ	Ⓓ	20.	Ⓐ	Ⓑ	Ⓒ	Ⓓ	26.	Ⓐ	Ⓑ	Ⓒ	Ⓓ
3.	Ⓐ	Ⓑ	Ⓒ	Ⓓ	9.	Ⓐ	Ⓑ	Ⓒ	Ⓓ	15.	Ⓐ	Ⓑ	Ⓒ	Ⓓ	21.	Ⓐ	Ⓑ	Ⓒ	Ⓓ	27.	Ⓐ	Ⓑ	Ⓒ	Ⓓ
4.	Ⓐ	Ⓑ	Ⓒ	Ⓓ	10.	Ⓐ	Ⓑ	Ⓒ	Ⓓ	16.	Ⓐ	Ⓑ	Ⓒ	Ⓓ	22.	Ⓐ	Ⓑ	Ⓒ	Ⓓ	28.	Ⓐ	Ⓑ	Ⓒ	Ⓓ
5.	Ⓐ	Ⓑ	Ⓒ	Ⓓ	11.	Ⓐ	Ⓑ	Ⓒ	Ⓓ	17.	Ⓐ	Ⓑ	Ⓒ	Ⓓ	23.	Ⓐ	Ⓑ	Ⓒ	Ⓓ	29.	Ⓐ	Ⓑ	Ⓒ	Ⓓ
6.	Ⓐ	Ⓑ	Ⓒ	Ⓓ	12.	Ⓐ	Ⓑ	Ⓒ	Ⓓ	18.	Ⓐ	Ⓑ	Ⓒ	Ⓓ	24.	Ⓐ	Ⓑ	Ⓒ	Ⓓ	30.	Ⓐ	Ⓑ	Ⓒ	Ⓓ

ADJECTIVES

LEARNING OBJECTIVES

➤ Adjectives of Quality
➤ Adjectives of Quantity

➤ Adjectives of Number
➤ Comparison of Adjectives

PRACTICE EXERCISE

I. Choose the correct adjectives from the alternatives given below and fill in the blanks:

1. This book is very ______.
    (A) informative
    (B) informing
    (C) informed
    (D) informs

2. She drew a very ________ diagram on the board.
    (A) confuse
    (B) confusing
    (C) confuses
    (D) confusive

3. Aman, your bedroom is ______. Please, tidy it up straight away.
    (A) disgrace
    (B) disgraced
    (C) disgracing
    (D) disgraceful

4. If you want to be good at football, you need a very ______ spirit.
    (A) compete
    (B) competition
    (C) competitive
    (D) competitor

5. This ball pen is ______. It has completely dried out.
    (A) use
    (B) useful
    (C) used
    (D) useless

6. It is not ______ to cycle down the busy main road.
    (A) advise
    (B) advising
    (C) advisable
    (D) advice

7. After a ______ week at work, Mrs. Batra enjoys a relaxing weekend with her family.
    (A) stress
    (B) stressed
    (C) stressing
    (D) stressful

8. The maths exam was ______ than I expected.
    (A) difficult
    (B) most difficult
    (C) least difficult
    (D) less difficult

9. Have you got _______ food?
   (A) little
   (B) less
   (C) some
   (D) any

10. Ajay is _______ than Amit.
    (A) taller
    (B) as tall as
    (C) the tallest
    (D) none of these

11. Television programs that are shown late at night are not always ________________.
    (A) suitable of children
    (B) suitable with children
    (C) suitable children
    (D) suitable for children

12. Sonia gave me a _______ recipe for cheesecake.
    (A) quick easy
    (B) quickly and easy
    (C) quick and easily
    (D) quick and easy

13. I'm going to throw out these old clothes. They're _______.
    (A) good for nothing
    (B) good at nothing
    (C) good with nothing
    (D) good of nothing

14. I made a painting yesterday. It was good but not _____ yours.
    (A) as good as
    (B) good as
    (C) better as
    (D) the good

15. I don't like _____ pop music I hate it all.
    (A) little
    (B) less
    (C) some
    (D) none of these

16. Pani is ________ than Samira.
    (A) more beautiful
    (B) as beautiful as
    (C) the most beautiful
    (D) none of these

17. Going to Disneyland was _____ day of my life.
    (A) the most exciting
    (B) most exciting
    (C) the most exciting
    (D) more exciting

18. You are _____ than my sister.
    (A) crazier
    (B) as crazy as
    (C) the craziest
    (D) none of these

19. I heard a noise. ________ body is outside.
    (A) Little
    (B) Less
    (C) Some
    (D) Any

20. ________ people don't like Bill Clinton.
    (A) Little
    (B) Less
    (C) Some
    (D) Any

21. Read the sentences and identify correct and incorrect and choose the correct option.
    (a) How farther do you plan to drive tonight?
    (b) Do you have any farther plans for adding on to the building?
    (c) I just can't go any further.
    (d) That's a lot further than I want to carry this heavy suitcase!
    (A) (a) and (b) are correct
    (B) (b) and (d) are correct
    (C) (c) and (d) are correct
    (D) (a) and (c) are correct

22. Read the sentences and identify correct and incorrect and choose the correct option.
    (a) My neighbours have a son and a daughter; the former is a teacher, the latter is a nurse.
    (b) I will address that at a later time.
    (c) Of the first two Harry Potter books. I prefer the later.
    (d) John arrived at the party latter than Mary did.
    (A) (a) and (b) are correct
    (B) (b) and (d) ore correct
    (C) (c) and (d) are correct
    (D) (a) and (c) are correct

23. Read the sentences and identify correct and incorrect and choose the correct option.
    (a) I have less than an hour to do this work.
    (b) There were fewer days below freezing last winter.
    (c) People these days are buying less newspapers.
    (d) I drank less water than she her.
    (A) (a) and (b) are correct
    (B) (a) and (d) are correct
    (C) (c) and (d) are correct
    (D) (a) and (c) are correct

24. Read the statements and choose true or false.
    Statement A: Out of chapters 1, 2, and 3, the latter one is the most difficult to learn.
    Statement B: Dan is now friends with Ruth, Maya and Ben. The last is his cousin.
    (A) TT (B) TF
    (C) FT (D) FF

25. From the choices provided after each sentence, select a word or phrase that would correctly complete the sentence. Uncle Carl is really ____________ man.
    (A) an old sweet
    (B) a sweet, old
    (C) a sweet old
    (D) none of the above

─── Darken Your Choice with HB Pencil ───

1.	A B C D	6.	A B C D	11.	A B C D	16	A B C D	21.	A B C D
2.	A B C D	7.	A B C D	12.	A B C D	17.	A B C D	22.	A B C D
3.	A B C D	8.	A B C D	13.	A B C D	18.	A B C D	23.	A B C D
4.	A B C D	9.	A B C D	14.	A B C D	19.	A B C D	24.	A B C D
5.	A B C D	10.	A B C D	15.	A B C D	20.	A B C D	25.	A B C D

ARTICLES

LEARNING OBJECTIVES

➤ Rules of Articles
➤ Omission of an Article

PRACTICE EXERCISE

I. Fill in the blanks with suitable article from the options given below:

1. _____ hotel.
   (A) An   (B) The
   (C) A   (D) None of these

2. Make sure you put your name at _____ end of the report.
   (A) an   (B) the
   (C) a   (D) None of these

3. Could you close _________ door, please? It's really cold.
   (A) an   (B) the
   (C) a   (D) None of these

4. We have got our new offices near _____ centre of the city.
   (A) an   (B) the
   (C) a   (D) None of these

5. For lunch I had _____ sandwich.
   (A) an   (B) the
   (C) a   (D) None of these

6. When you come out of the lift, you'll see two doors, _____ red one and _____ blue one. My door is _____ red one.
   (A) The/the/a   (B) A/a/the
   (C) A/a/a   (D) The/the/the

7. We need to do more for _______ poor.
   (A) an   (B) the
   (C) a   (D) None of these

8. The greatest invention of the 20th century is _____ computer.
   (A) an   (B) the
   (C) a   (C) None of these

9. I'm looking for _____ new job.
   (A) an   (B) the
   (C) a   (D) None of these

10. I saw_____ man going into the office. I don't know who _____ man was.
   (A) An/the   (B) The/a
   (C) a/the   (D) a/a

11. _______ British Airways is one of the oldest companies of the world.
   (A) An   (B) The
   (C) A   (D) None of these

12. _____ World Bank is a big organisation.
   (A) An   (B) The
   (C) A   (D) None of these

13. There is a box of sweets on _____ table.
   (A) a   (B) an
   (C) the   (D) None of these

OLYMPIAD WORKBOOK (IEO) CLASS– 5

14. When we arrived, she went straight to the kitchen and started to prepare _____ meal for us.
    (A) a   (B) an
    (C) the   (D) None of these
15. Mt. Everest is __________ highest mountain in the world.
    (A) a   (B) an
    (C) the   (D) None of these
16. Do you like _____ weather here? Isn't it too hot during _____ day?
    (A) a/a   (B) an/a
    (C) the/the   (D) none of these

17. Rustum is _____ young parsee.
    (A) a   (B) an
    (C) the   (D) None of these
18. Varanasi is _____ holy city.
    (A) a   (B) an
    (C) the   (D) None of these
19. The world is _____ happy place.
    (A) a   (B) an
    (C) the   (D) None of these
20. _____ sun shines brightly.
    (A) A   (B) An
    (C) The   (D) None of these

HOTS (ACHIEVERS SECTION)

Fill in the blanks with suitable article from the options given below:

21. _____ Children recited _____ poem in _____ honour of _____ Prime Minister.
    (A) the, a, an, a
    (B) a, the, the, the
    (C) no article, a, an, the
    (D) the, a, the, the
22. There is _____ fish in _____ bottle.
    (A) the, the
    (B) a, the
    (C) a, a
    (D) none
23. I saw _____ good deal of him during _____ war.

    (A) no article, a   (B) the, the
    (C) a, a   (D) a, the
24. We missed our train because we were waiting on _____ wrong platform. We were on _____ Platform 3 instead of _____ Platform 8.
    (A) the, the, the
    (B) the, no article, no article
    (C) no article, no article, no article
    (D) the, a, a
25. _____ Wisdom is _____ great virtue.
    (A) the, the   (B) a, the
    (C) an, the   (D) no article, a

PREPOSITIONS

LEARNING OBJECTIVES

- ➤ Simple Prepositions
- ➤ Double Prepositions
- ➤ Phrase Prepositions
- ➤ Compound Prepositions
- ➤ Participle Prepositions

PRACTICE EXERCISE

I. Fill in the blanks with the most suitable collocation.

1. It is _______ seven o' clock in the evening.
    - (A) across
    - (B) along
    - (C) about
    - (D) among

2. Rahul is _______ such mean behaviour.
    - (A) across
    - (B) above
    - (C) after
    - (D) among

3. She is leaning _______ the wall.
    - (A) across
    - (B) amid
    - (C) at
    - (D) against

4. The students entered the hall in a line one _______ the other.
    - (A) after
    - (B) along
    - (C) around
    - (D) by

5. The teacher distributed the question papers _______ the students.
    - (A) across
    - (B) around
    - (C) about
    - (D) among

6. His office is right _______ the road.
    - (A) across
    - (B) after
    - (C) about
    - (D) after

7. The train is running _______ its scheduled time.
    - (A) besides
    - (B) behind
    - (C) down
    - (D) below

8. It is nice and warm to sit _______ fire in the winters.
    - (A) but
    - (B) by
    - (C) of
    - (D) for

9. River Yamuna flows_______ Ganges in Allahabad.
    - (A) into
    - (B) in
    - (C) from
    - (D) between

10. Rita is not _______ the house.
    - (A) of
    - (B) from
    - (C) in
    - (D) by

II. Choose the correct option from the given alternatives.

11. What is the distance between/beyond Delhi and Jaipur?

12. The rain ruined all but/by one painting.

13. She stood under/behind the tree to avoid rain.

14. He reached the theatre before/behind time in his eagerness.

15. The criminal was punished with imprisonment for/in life.

16. Alexander was the youngest among/around his generals.

17. The bags of sand were set along/across the banks to prevent the river from flooding.

18. Sunita is fond of/about the flute.
19. He slept late into/in the day.
20. During monsoons, rivers often flow above/about the danger mark.

III. Choose the most appropriate preposition from the box and fill in the blanks.

Without, Up, Through, Towards, With, To, Under, Over, Off, Within

21. He fell __________ his horse.
22. The sun shines __________ the earth.
23. The chances of victory are three __________ one.
24. He worked very hard __________ the year to secure first rank.
25. She was very kind __________ her neighbours.

HOTS (ACHIEVERS SECTION)

Fill in the blanks with correct preposition.

26. Don't forget to bring some flowers _______ you.
27. You can look up the word _______ a dictionary.
28. She is allergic _______ insect stings.
29. The song was sung _______ Lata Mangeshkar.
30. The police car chased the robbers _______ the streets.

1.	Ⓐ Ⓑ Ⓒ Ⓓ	7.	Ⓐ Ⓑ Ⓒ Ⓓ	13.	Ⓐ Ⓑ Ⓒ Ⓓ	19	Ⓐ Ⓑ Ⓒ Ⓓ	25.	Ⓐ Ⓑ Ⓒ Ⓓ
2.	Ⓐ Ⓑ Ⓒ Ⓓ	8.	Ⓐ Ⓑ Ⓒ Ⓓ	14.	Ⓐ Ⓑ Ⓒ Ⓓ	20.	Ⓐ Ⓑ Ⓒ Ⓓ	26.	Ⓐ Ⓑ Ⓒ Ⓓ
3.	Ⓐ Ⓑ Ⓒ Ⓓ	9.	Ⓐ Ⓑ Ⓒ Ⓓ	15.	Ⓐ Ⓑ Ⓒ Ⓓ	21.	Ⓐ Ⓑ Ⓒ Ⓓ	27.	Ⓐ Ⓑ Ⓒ Ⓓ
4.	Ⓐ Ⓑ Ⓒ Ⓓ	10.	Ⓐ Ⓑ Ⓒ Ⓓ	16.	Ⓐ Ⓑ Ⓒ Ⓓ	22.	Ⓐ Ⓑ Ⓒ Ⓓ	28.	Ⓐ Ⓑ Ⓒ Ⓓ
5.	Ⓐ Ⓑ Ⓒ Ⓓ	11.	Ⓐ Ⓑ Ⓒ Ⓓ	17.	Ⓐ Ⓑ Ⓒ Ⓓ	23.	Ⓐ Ⓑ Ⓒ Ⓓ	29.	Ⓐ Ⓑ Ⓒ Ⓓ
6.	Ⓐ Ⓑ Ⓒ Ⓓ	12.	Ⓐ Ⓑ Ⓒ Ⓓ	18.	Ⓐ Ⓑ Ⓒ Ⓓ	24.	Ⓐ Ⓑ Ⓒ Ⓓ	30.	Ⓐ Ⓑ Ⓒ Ⓓ

CONJUNCTIONS

LEARNING OBJECTIVES

➤ Conjunction to connects words, phrases or clauses

PRACTICE EXERCISE

1. Luisa waked with extreme precision, -- that served her well in her law career.
   (A) A meticulousness (B) An effrontery
   (C) An inhibition (D) A litigiousness
2. Choose the option that best fills in the blank:
   She prefers living in cities such _____ New York or London.
   (A) that (B) than
   (C) as (D) for
3. Choose the correct option to fill the blank:
   He is so weak _____ he cannot walk
   (A) but (B) that
   (C) then (D) so
4. Directions For Questions
   Read the following conversation and choose the appropriate option to fill in theblanks:
   Arvind: I've just started going to a new gym.
   Shobha: Oh, really? Me ____ (1)_____. Which gym?
   Arvind: It's called Fitlife.
   Shobha: That's not my gym. _____ (2)_____, I've heard of it and the trainer.
   Arvind: I don't like the trainer _____ (3)_____ the decor is great!
   Shobha: My friends say he's _____ (4)_____ hard of hearing or rude.
   Arvind: I don't know. I've only been twice.

   Fill in blank (3).
   (A) And (B) But
   (C) In spite of (D) Even
5. Choose the option that best fills the blank:
   No sooner had I received her text, _____ I left for her house.
   (A) but (B) than
   (C) when (D) for
6. Combine the sentences using the conjunctions 'so...that':
   Mike is ill. The doctors suspect he may not survive.
   (A) Mike is ill so that the doctors suspect he may not survive.
   (B) Mike is so ill the doctors suspect that he may not survive.
   (C) Mike is so ill that the doctors suspect he may not survive.
   (D) Mike was that ill so the doctors suspect he may not survive.
7. Combine the sentences correctly using 'so...that':
   He is tall. He does not fit in the car.
   (A) He is tall so that he does not fit in the car.
   (B) He is so tall that he does not fit in the car.
   (C) He is so that tall, he does not fit in the car.
   (D) So he is tall that he does not fit in the car.

8. Combine the sentences correctly using 'so...that':
David is short. He can't reach the top of the shelf.
(A) David is so short that he can't reach the top of the shelf.
(B) David is short so that he can't reach the top of the shelf.
(C) David is that short so he can't reach the top of the shelf.
(D) So that David is short, he can't reach the top of the shelf.

9. Combine the sentences correctly using 'so...that':

The hill was steep. We couldn't climb to the top.
(A) So steep the hill was that we couldn't climb to the top.
(B) The hill was steep so that we couldn't climb to the top.
(C) The hill was so steep that we couldn't climb to the top.
(D) That the hill was so steep we couldn't climb to the top.

10. Identify the correct word to fill in the blank:

He left the show so ______ he could practice for the audition.
(A) that   (B) then
(C) as   (D) because

11. Combine the sentences correctly using 'so...that':
The earrings were beautiful. I had to buy them.
(A) The earrings were so beautiful that I had to buy them.
(B) The earrings were beautiful so that I had to buy them.
(C) So beautiful were the earrings that I had to buy them.
(D) So that the earrings were beautiful that I had to buy them.

12. Combine the sentences correctly using 'so...that':

James is arrogant. He would never ask for help.
(A) James is so arrogant that he would never ask for help.
(B) James is arrogant so that he would never ask for help.
(C) So arrogant James is that he would never ask for help.
(D) That James is so arrogant he would never ask for help.

13. Combine the sentences correctly using 'so...that':
It was cold. We couldn't play outdoors.
(A) It was so cold that we couldn't play outdoors.
(B) It was cold so that we couldn't play outdoors.
(C) We couldn't play outdoors so that it was cold.
(D) We couldn't play outdoors that it was so cold.

14. Combine the sentences correctly using 'so ... that':
It was bright. It hurt my eyes.
(A) It was bright so that it hurt my eyes.
(B) It was so bright that it hurt my eyes.
(C) It was that bright so it hurt my eyes.
(D) So bright it was that it hurt my eyes.

15. Choose the option that best fills the blank:
No sooner did she read his letter ____ she fainted.
(A) than   (B) but
(C) after   (D) when

16. Choose the option that best fills the blank:
No sooner had she finished her task, ______ she started the next one.
(A) but   (B) than
(C) when   (D) after

17. Choose the option that best fills the blank:
No sooner did the child start crying ____ his father lifted him up.
(A) then   (B) but
(C) after   (D) than

18. Choose the option that best fills the blank:

No sooner had she finished her task,______ she started the next one.

(A) but   (B) than
(C) when   (D) after

19. Choose the option that best fills the blank:

No sooner had they completed their work, ______ they asked for their salaries.

(A) for   (B) but
(C) than   (D) when

20. Choose the option that best fills the blank:

No sooner did I take a dose of aspirin ______ I started feeling better.

(A) after   (B) than
(C) then   (D) when

HOTS (ACHIEVERS SECTION)

21. Choose the option that best fills the blank:

No sooner did he reach the train station _____ the train arrived.

(A) than   (B) after
(C) for   (D) then

22. Choose the option that best fills the blank:

No sooner did the professor enter the classroom ______ the students stood up.

(A) then   (B) than
(C) for   (D) after

23. Fill in the blank with a suitable option:

We decided to stay out all night ______ that we could watch the stars.

(A) and   (B) because
(C) so   (D) after

24. Choose the option that best fills in the blank:

Joseph worked all night __________ that he could get his work done before the deadline.

(A) so   (B) and
(C) after   (D) that

25. Choose the option that best fills in the blank:

You'd better drink lots of water when you go trekking ______ that you don't get dehydrated.

(A) after   (B) and
(C) for   (D) so

Darken Your Choice with HB Pencil

1. Ⓐ Ⓑ Ⓒ Ⓓ	6. Ⓐ Ⓑ Ⓒ Ⓓ	11. Ⓐ Ⓑ Ⓒ Ⓓ	16 Ⓐ Ⓑ Ⓒ Ⓓ	21. Ⓐ Ⓑ Ⓒ Ⓓ
2. Ⓐ Ⓑ Ⓒ Ⓓ	7. Ⓐ Ⓑ Ⓒ Ⓓ	12. Ⓐ Ⓑ Ⓒ Ⓓ	17. Ⓐ Ⓑ Ⓒ Ⓓ	22. Ⓐ Ⓑ Ⓒ Ⓓ
3. Ⓐ Ⓑ Ⓒ Ⓓ	8. Ⓐ Ⓑ Ⓒ Ⓓ	13. Ⓐ Ⓑ Ⓒ Ⓓ	18. Ⓐ Ⓑ Ⓒ Ⓓ	23. Ⓐ Ⓑ Ⓒ Ⓓ
4. Ⓐ Ⓑ Ⓒ Ⓓ	9. Ⓐ Ⓑ Ⓒ Ⓓ	14. Ⓐ Ⓑ Ⓒ Ⓓ	19. Ⓐ Ⓑ Ⓒ Ⓓ	24. Ⓐ Ⓑ Ⓒ Ⓓ
5. Ⓐ Ⓑ Ⓒ Ⓓ	10. Ⓐ Ⓑ Ⓒ Ⓓ	15. Ⓐ Ⓑ Ⓒ Ⓓ	20. Ⓐ Ⓑ Ⓒ Ⓓ	25. Ⓐ Ⓑ Ⓒ Ⓓ

TENSES

LEARNING OBJECTIVES

➤ Simple Tenses

➤ Perfect Tenses

➤ Continuous Tense

PRACTICE EXERCISE

I. Put in the verbs given in brackets into the blanks using Simple Tense.

1. The boys _____________ hockey at school. (to play)

2. She _____________ e-mails. (not to write)

3. _____________ you _____________ English? (to speak)

4. My parents _____________ fish. (not to like)

5. When _____________ you _____________ this wonderful skirt? (to design)

6. My mother _____________ into the van. (not to crash)

7. The boys _____________ the mudguards of their bicycles. (to take off)

8. They_____________ back by 6:30 pm. (to be)

9. _____________ you _____________ me? (to help)

10. We _____________ sweets. (not to buy)

II. Put in the verbs given in brackets into the blanks using Continuous Tense.

11. We _____________ the checkpoint. (not to pass)

12. _____________ they _____________ to help? (to try)

13. She _____________ to the centre of the town. (not to walk)

14. She _____________ a heavy bag. (to carry)

15. _____________when someone stole your clothes? (you/not/to/swim)

16. _____________ you _____________ during the last lesson? (to yawn)

17. They _____________ stickers. (to swap)

18. Tomorrow at nine I _____________ a test. (to write)

19. You _____________ pizza soon. (to eat)

20. We _____________ him tomorrow. (to meet)

III. Put in the verbs given in brackets into the blanks using Continuous Tense.

21. _____________ the whole morning? (she to walk)

22. Who _____________ in the garden? (to dig)

23. They _____________. (not to cycle)

24. Hari _____________ this book, but Richa has. (not to read)

25. I _____________ there for more than three hours when she finally arrived. (wait)

"

26. Rewrite the following sentences in the tenses mentioned.

(A) Megha is eating cake.

1. Simple Present:

2. Simple Past:

3. Past Continuous:

(B) I read a book on Delhi's history.

1. Past Perfect:

2. Past Continuous:

3. Present Perfect Continuous:

1.	Ⓐ Ⓑ Ⓒ Ⓓ	7.	Ⓐ Ⓑ Ⓒ Ⓓ	13.	Ⓐ Ⓑ Ⓒ Ⓓ	19	Ⓐ Ⓑ Ⓒ Ⓓ	25.	Ⓐ Ⓑ Ⓒ Ⓓ
2.	Ⓐ Ⓑ Ⓒ Ⓓ	8.	Ⓐ Ⓑ Ⓒ Ⓓ	14.	Ⓐ Ⓑ Ⓒ Ⓓ	20.	Ⓐ Ⓑ Ⓒ Ⓓ	26.	Ⓐ Ⓑ Ⓒ Ⓓ
3.	Ⓐ Ⓑ Ⓒ Ⓓ	9.	Ⓐ Ⓑ Ⓒ Ⓓ	15.	Ⓐ Ⓑ Ⓒ Ⓓ	21.	Ⓐ Ⓑ Ⓒ Ⓓ		
4.	Ⓐ Ⓑ Ⓒ Ⓓ	10.	Ⓐ Ⓑ Ⓒ Ⓓ	16.	Ⓐ Ⓑ Ⓒ Ⓓ	22.	Ⓐ Ⓑ Ⓒ Ⓓ		
5.	Ⓐ Ⓑ Ⓒ Ⓓ	11.	Ⓐ Ⓑ Ⓒ Ⓓ	17.	Ⓐ Ⓑ Ⓒ Ⓓ	23.	Ⓐ Ⓑ Ⓒ Ⓓ		
6.	Ⓐ Ⓑ Ⓒ Ⓓ	12.	Ⓐ Ⓑ Ⓒ Ⓓ	18.	Ⓐ Ⓑ Ⓒ Ⓓ	24.	Ⓐ Ⓑ Ⓒ Ⓓ		

JUMBLED WORDS

LEARNING OBJECTIVES

➤ Jumbled words
➤ Jumbled sentences

PRACTICE EXERCISE

1. Rearrange the words to make a meaningful sentence:

    summer / is / in / it / wonderful / hills / to / to / go / the

    (A) To go to hills it is wonderful in the summer.

    (B) It is wonderful to go to the hills in summer.

    (C) In the summer to go to hills it is wonderful.

    (D) It is wonderful in the summer to go to hills.

2. Rearrange the words to make a meaningful sentence:

    rules / one / by / must / abide / the

    (A) Rules must abide by the one.

    (B) The rules by one must abide.

    (C) One must abide by the rules.

    (D) One the rules by abide must.

3. Rearrange the words to make a meaningful sentence:

    could / accident / few / unhurt / from / escape / the / fire

    (A) Few could escape unhurt from the fire accident.

    (B) From the fire accident few could escape unhurt.

    (C) The fire accident few could escape unhurt from.

    (D) Unhurt escape could few from the fire accident.

4. Rearrange the words to make a meaningful sentence:

    many / anyone /I / were / there / but / not / know / did

    (A) I did not know anyone but many were there.

    (B) There were many I not know anyone but did

    (C) Many were there but I did not know anyone.

    (D) But I did not know anyone were many there.

5. Rearrange the words to make a meaningful sentence:

    ? / whose / house / is / this

    (A) Whose is this house?

    (B) Whose this house is?

    (C) Whose house is this?

    (D) This house is whose?

6. Rearrange the words to make a meaningful sentence:

    stood / first / term / first / who / the / in / class / ? / in

(A) First who stood in the class in first term?

(B) Who stood first in the class in first term?

(C) Who in stood first in the first term class?

(D) In class in the first term who stood first?

7. Rearrange the words to make a meaningful sentence:

pen / me / is / gave / you / beautiful / the /very

(A) The pen you gave me is very beautiful.

(B) You gave me the pen is very beautiful.

(C) The pen is very beautiful you gave me.

(D) You gave me pen is the very beautiful.

8. Rearrange the words to make a meaningful sentence:

my / English / teacher / is / Sheena

(A) My teacher English is Sheena.

(B) My teacher is Sheena English.

(C) Sheena is my English teacher.

(D) English teacher is my Sheena.

9. Rearrange the words to make a meaningful sentence:

helps / who / help / God / those / themselves /only

(A) Only God helps those help who themselves.

(B) God only helps those who help themselves.

(C) Who help themselves those God only helps.

(D) Those who help themselves helps only God.

10. Rearrange the words to make a meaningful sentence:

listen / what / to / parents / your / say

(A) What your parents say listen to.

(B) Your parents say listen to what.

(C) Listen to what your parents say

(D) Say what your parents listen to.

Directions: Rearrange the letters to make a meaningful word:

11. TENISNART

(A) Transent   (B) Transient

(C) Transeent   (D) Transeint

12. OLIPT

(A) Tolip   (B) Pilot

(C) Ploit   (D) Ploti

13. GNINIAMER

(A) Remaning   (B) Remaiening

(C) Remaining   (D) Remianing

14. NERDLIHC

(A) Childran   (B) Childrin

(C) Children   (D) All of these

15. HPYUAPN

(A) Unhapy   (B) Unpappy

(C) Unhayppy   (D) Unhappy

16. TPECAC

(A) Acept   (B) Accept

(C) Accepat   (D) All of these

17. EGABRAG

(A) Gargage   (B) Garbige

(C) Garbage   (D) Barbage

18. YEKNOM

(A) Monkay   (B) Monzey

(C) Mynoje   (D) Monkey

19. LLYI

(A) Lyli   (B) Liyl

(C) Lily   (D) Lili

20. YLWOLS

(A) Slowly

(B) Slowley

(C) Slowaly

(D) All of these

21. Rearrange the words to make a meaningful sentence:

    horse / has / the / hurt / itself
    (A) Horse has hurt the itself.
    (B) Itself has the horse hurt.
    (C) The horse has hurt itself.
    (D) Hurt itself has the horse.

22. Rearrange the words to make a meaningful sentence:

    poor / man / laughed / the / boys / at / the
    (A) The Boys laughed at the poor man.
    (B) Poor the man laughed the at boys.
    (C) The Poor man laughed the boys at.
    (D) Man the laughed at the poor boys.

23. Rearrange the words to make a meaningful sentence:

    situated / where / is / Nepal / ?
    (A) Where Nepal is situated?
    (B) Where is Nepal situated?
    (C) Where situated is Nepal?
    (D) Is where Nepal situated?

24. Rearrange the words to make a meaningful sentence:

    has / hung / wall / on / the / who / painting / the / ?
    (A) Hung who has the painting on the wall?
    (B) Has who hung the painting on the wall?
    (C) Who has hung the painting on the wall?
    (D) Who hung has the painting on the wall?

25. Rearrange the words to make a meaningful sentence:

    don't / have /1 / money / enough
    (A) Enough money don't have I.
    (B) I don't have enough money
    (C) I have don't enough money
    (D) Don't have enough money

—Darken Your Choice with HB Pencil—

1.	Ⓐ Ⓑ Ⓒ Ⓓ	6.	Ⓐ Ⓑ Ⓒ Ⓓ	11.	Ⓐ Ⓑ Ⓒ Ⓓ	16	Ⓐ Ⓑ Ⓒ Ⓓ	21.	Ⓐ Ⓑ Ⓒ Ⓓ
2.	Ⓐ Ⓑ Ⓒ Ⓓ	7.	Ⓐ Ⓑ Ⓒ Ⓓ	12.	Ⓐ Ⓑ Ⓒ Ⓓ	17.	Ⓐ Ⓑ Ⓒ Ⓓ	22.	Ⓐ Ⓑ Ⓒ Ⓓ
3.	Ⓐ Ⓑ Ⓒ Ⓓ	8.	Ⓐ Ⓑ Ⓒ Ⓓ	13.	Ⓐ Ⓑ Ⓒ Ⓓ	18.	Ⓐ Ⓑ Ⓒ Ⓓ	23.	Ⓐ Ⓑ Ⓒ Ⓓ
4.	Ⓐ Ⓑ Ⓒ Ⓓ	9.	Ⓐ Ⓑ Ⓒ Ⓓ	14.	Ⓐ Ⓑ Ⓒ Ⓓ	19.	Ⓐ Ⓑ Ⓒ Ⓓ	24.	Ⓐ Ⓑ Ⓒ Ⓓ
5.	Ⓐ Ⓑ Ⓒ Ⓓ	10.	Ⓐ Ⓑ Ⓒ Ⓓ	15.	Ⓐ Ⓑ Ⓒ Ⓓ	20.	Ⓐ Ⓑ Ⓒ Ⓓ	25.	Ⓐ Ⓑ Ⓒ Ⓓ

VOICE AND NARRATION 

LEARNING OBJECTIVES

➤ Active and passive Voice
➤ Fundamental rules of Indirect Speech

PRACTICE EXERCISE

Choose the correct option (form of verb) and fill in the blanks.

1. At the new Chinese restaurant, when you have finished your meal, you _______ a cup of special tea.
   (A) give (B) are giving
   (C) are given (D) gave

2. _______ glass _______ from sand?
   (A) Does/ made (B) Is/made
   (C) Is/making (D) Is/make

3. If this dish _______ today, I will throw it out.
   (A) doesn't finish (B) isn't finish
   (C) isn't finishing (D) isn't finished

4. The plans for the new school _______ yet.
   (A) aren't finish (B) aren't finishing
   (C) didn't finish (D) aren't finished

5. Are you going to the party? No, we _______.
   (A) aren't invite (B) aren't invited
   (C) didn't invite (D) aren't inviting

6. The front of the building _______ in a very nice colour.
   (A) didn't paint (B) isn't paint
   (C) isn't painted (D) isn't painting

7. Our garbage _______ twice a week.
   (A) is collect (B) collecting
   (C) is collected (D) are collected

8. The grass _______ yesterday. It looks lovely.
   (A) was cutting (B) were cutting
   (C) was cut (D) were cut

9. Twenty more trees _______ in the school garden last year.
   (A) were planting (B) were planted
   (C) was planted (D) was planting

10. The stolen jewellery _______ until the robbers confessed.
    (A) wasn't find (B) wasn't finding
    (C) wasn't found (D) didn't find

11. The trucks _______ at the border by the customs officers.
    (A) wasn't stopped
    (B) weren't stopping
    (C) weren't stop
    (D) weren't stopped

12. The floor _______ early this morning.
    (A) were sweep (B) were swept
    (C) was swept (D) was sweep

13. A treat _______ to celebrate the wonderful news.
    (A) was gave
    (B) was give
    (C) was giving
    (D) was given

OLYMPIAD WORKBOOK (IEO) CLASS— 5

14. The computer _________ in the 2000s, but much earlier.
   (A) wasn't invent
   (B) weren't invited
   (C) wasn't invented
   (D) wasn't inventing
15. I was surprised by the size of their house. I ______ there before.
   (A) had never been
   (B) have never been
   (C) was never been
   (D) did never be

II. Choose the correct option that shows transformation of the following sentences in to indirect narration and vice-versa.

16. She said, 'I shall come in a few minutes.'
   (A) She said he will come.
   (B) She said that she would come in a few minutes.
   (C) She said I will come.
   (D) I will come he said.
17. John said, 'It is raining very heavily outside.'
   (A) John said it is raining very heavily outside.
   (B) It is raining very heavily outside John said.
   (C) John said that it was raining very heavily outside.
   (D) John said that it rained very heavily outside.
18. Maria said to me, 'Please save my life.'
   (A) Please save her life she said.
   (B) My life please save she said to me.
   (C) Maria said to save her life.
   (D) Maria requested me to save her life.
19. The boss said to him, 'Do you notice any change?'
   (A) The boss asked him if he noticed any change.
   (B) The boss said did he notice any change.

(C) He asked if he find any change.
(D) To him the boss said if he find any change.
20. Imran said to her, 'Obey your seniors.'
   (A) Imran said her to obey seniors.
   (B) Imran advised her to obey her seniors.
   (C) Seniors should be obeyed he told her.
   (D) He asked if she obey her seniors.
21. 'How old is your mother?' he asked.
   (A) He asked how old her mother was.
   (B) She asked how old his mother was.
   (C) I asked how old your mother was.
   (D) She asked how your mother is now.
22. Peter said to John, 'Why are you so late?'
   (A) Peter asked John why he was so late.
   (B) John asked Peter why he was so late.
   (C) Peter asked John why was he late.
   (D) John asked Peter why was he late.
23. 'Are you British or American?'
   (A) He asked me whether I was British or American.
   (B) He asked me was I British or American.
   (C) British or American, he asked me who am I.
   (D) He asked me I was British or American.
24. Where are you going?
   (A) She asked where I was going.
   (B) She asked am I going anywhere.
   (C) She enquired was I going anywhere.
   (D) She asked was I going anywhere.
25. He said, 'I like this song.'
   (A) He said that he would like this song.
   (B) He said that he liked that song.
   (C) He said that he would like that song.
   (D) He said that he will like this song.

26. Use the information given in the headlines to complete the sentence, from the options given below: "4 Robbers caught and arrested". The police ________ 4 robbers from Rohini sector 11 for stealing valuables.
    (A) has been caught and arrested
    (B) have caught and arrested
    (C) are catching and arresting
    (D) were catching and arresting

27. Complete the following paragraph with passive form of verb given in the brackets from the options below; The birthday of Mahatma Gandhi __(2)__ (celebrate) all over the country. He__(3)__ (known) as 'Bapu or 'father of the nation'. Gandhiji __(4)__ (love) and __(5)__ by millions of Indians even today.
    (A) being celebrated
    (B) was celebrate
    (C) celebrated
    (D) is celebrated

28. Complete the following paragraph with passive form of verb given in the brackets from the options below; The birthday of Mahatma Gandhi __(2)__ (celebrate) all over the country. He__(3)__ (known) as 'Bapu or 'father of the nation'. Gandhiji __(4)__ (love) and __(5)__ by millions of Indians even today.
    (A) is known
    (B) was known
    (C) has known
    (D) has been known

I. **Choose the correct option that shows transformation of the following sentences in to indirect narration and vice-versa.**

29. She said, 'I shall come in a few minutes.'
    (A) She said he will come.
    (B) She said that she would come in a few minutes.
    (C) She said I will come.
    (D) I will come he said.

30. John said, 'It is raining very heavily outside.'
    (A) John said it is raining very heavily outside.
    (B) It is raining very heavily outside John said.
    (C) John said that it was raining very heavily outside.
    (D) John said that it rained very heavily outside.

Darken Your Choice with HB Pencil

1.	Ⓐ Ⓑ Ⓒ Ⓓ	7.	Ⓐ Ⓑ Ⓒ Ⓓ	13.	Ⓐ Ⓑ Ⓒ Ⓓ	19	Ⓐ Ⓑ Ⓒ Ⓓ	25.	Ⓐ Ⓑ Ⓒ Ⓓ
2.	Ⓐ Ⓑ Ⓒ Ⓓ	8.	Ⓐ Ⓑ Ⓒ Ⓓ	14.	Ⓐ Ⓑ Ⓒ Ⓓ	20.	Ⓐ Ⓑ Ⓒ Ⓓ	26.	Ⓐ Ⓑ Ⓒ Ⓓ
3.	Ⓐ Ⓑ Ⓒ Ⓓ	9.	Ⓐ Ⓑ Ⓒ Ⓓ	15.	Ⓐ Ⓑ Ⓒ Ⓓ	21.	Ⓐ Ⓑ Ⓒ Ⓓ	27.	Ⓐ Ⓑ Ⓒ Ⓓ
4.	Ⓐ Ⓑ Ⓒ Ⓓ	10.	Ⓐ Ⓑ Ⓒ Ⓓ	16.	Ⓐ Ⓑ Ⓒ Ⓓ	22.	Ⓐ Ⓑ Ⓒ Ⓓ	28.	Ⓐ Ⓑ Ⓒ Ⓓ
5.	Ⓐ Ⓑ Ⓒ Ⓓ	11.	Ⓐ Ⓑ Ⓒ Ⓓ	17.	Ⓐ Ⓑ Ⓒ Ⓓ	23.	Ⓐ Ⓑ Ⓒ Ⓓ	29.	Ⓐ Ⓑ Ⓒ Ⓓ
6.	Ⓐ Ⓑ Ⓒ Ⓓ	12.	Ⓐ Ⓑ Ⓒ Ⓓ	18.	Ⓐ Ⓑ Ⓒ Ⓓ	24.	Ⓐ Ⓑ Ⓒ Ⓓ	30.	Ⓐ Ⓑ Ⓒ Ⓓ

READING COMPREHENSION

➤ Tips to Improve Reading Comprehension

PRACTICE EXERCISE

I. **Dreams do come true: The story of, the ball boy who became a World Cup winner**

On June 25, 1983, the Indian team had won the ICC World Cup (WC) and images of the team holding the trophy were inspirational for the entire nation.

I was just ten years of age and have fond memories of that victory. My parents allowed me to celebrate the victory till late in the night. I was also inspired to take up playing the game with the season (hard) ball after the World Cup victory. My first 'live' piece of World Cup action was during the 1987 edition, which was co-hosted by India and Pakistan. I was fortunate to be among the volunteers to be picked as a ball boy for the matches played in Mumbai. As I stood there watching the Indian greats on the field, I kept telling myself that I needed to be a part of the action in the middle.

In 1992, I made my maiden appearance in the match against England in Perth. Since then, I went on to play many matches and met many ups and downs, both professionally and personally. 2003 was the closest I had come, till then, to lift the coveted trophy. The most forgettable Cup for me has to be the 2007 edition in the West Indies. The early exit from the tournament ranks among the worst moments of my cricketing career.

The disappointment in the tournament served as a boost to prove many naysayers wrong. I spoke to the media about looking forward to 2011 tournament and 'being able to achieve what we want to achieve'. As the tournament progressed, we did worry our fans in the group stage with our performance but started generating momentum as we entered the quarter finals.

In defeating top sides like Australia, Pakistan and eventually overcoming Sri Lanka in the final, India emerged as the first nation to win the World Cup on home soil. It was even more special as I had finally been part of the winning team after 22 years of pursuit. The victory in 2011 was the highest point of my career as a nation unified in its celebrations.

Answer the following questions in not more than 20 words.

1. How does the speaker remember the World Cup victory of 1983?

2. Did the speaker participate in the 1987 tournament and in what capacity?

3. How is the 1992 World Cup important for the speaker?

4. How is the 2007 World Cup described?

5. What is the importance of 2011 World Cup for the speaker and the history of the tournament?

II.   Movie Plot: Hachi

In a school, students are giving oral presentations about personal heroes. Ronnie's subject is his grandfather's dog.

Years earlier, a puppy is sent from Japan to the United States, but escapes when his cage falls at an American train station. Professor Parker Wilson finds the dog and takes it home with the intention of returning the animal to its owner. His wife, Cate Parker, does not want them to keep the puppy. The following morning, he takes him to work, where Ken, a Japanese professor and colleague, translates the symbol on the collar as 'Hachi'—Japanese for the number 8— signifying good fortune. Parker decides to call the dog Hachiko. Cate receives a call from someone wishing to adopt the puppy, but having seen how close her husband is with Hachi, she declines.

Parker continues to be mystified by Hachi's refusal to do dog-like activities. One morning, Parker leaves for work and Hachi follows him to the train station; he refuses to leave until Parker walks him home. Later in the afternoon, Hachi walks to the station, to wait patiently for Parker to come home. Parker relents and walks Hachi to the station every morning. After Parker's train departs, Hachi walks home, returning in the afternoon to see his master's train arrive and go home together. They continue to do this every day.

One day Parker gets ready to leave and Hachi barks at him and refuses to join him. When Parker does leave, Hachi chases him while holding his ball. Not wishing to be late, Parker catches his train despite Hachi's barking. Later that day Parker is teaching, still holding Hachi's ball, when he suddenly suffers a heart attack and dies.

At the train station, Hachi waits patiently as the train arrives, but there is no sign of Parker. He remains, lying in the snow, for several hours, until Parker's son-in-law Michael comes for him. As time passes, Cate sells the house and Hachi is sent to live with her daughter Andy, Michael and their baby Ronnie. However, at the first opportunity, Hachi escapes and goes back to the station, where he sits at his usual spot. Andy arrives and takes him home, but lets him out the next day to return to the station.

For the next ten years, Hachi waits for his owner. His loyalty is profiled in the local newspaper. Cate comes back to visit Parker's grave where she meets Ken. Walking past the station, she is stunned to see Hachi maintaining his vigil. Overcome with grief, Cate sits and waits for the next train with him. At home, Cate tells the now ten-year-old Ronnie about Hachi. Hachi continues his daily walk to the same spot in front of the train station to his final day when he recollects his life with his master.

Answer the following questions in not more than 20 words.

6. Who is narrating the story and why?

____

____

____

7. Why does Professor Wilson name the dog Hachiko?

____

____

____

8. Who is Ken?

____

____

____

9. What extraordinary behaviour does Hachi show towards his master?

____

____

____

10. Why is Hachi's story profiled in the newspaper?

____

____

____

III. US space society award for ISRO for the Mars mission

Indian Space Research Organisation (ISRO) has been conferred the 'Space Pioneer Award' by the National Space Society (NSS) of the United States over the historic feat on successfully sending a satellite on a orbit to Martian atmosphere in its very first attempt.

The award would be presented to an ISRO representative during the 34th Annual International Space Development Conference to be held at Toronto in Canada.

The 'Space Pioneer Award' consists of a silvery pewter Moon globe cast by the Baker Art Foundry in Placerville, California, from a sculpture originally created by well-known space and astronomical artist.

The mission has achieved two mission firsts. (1) An Indian spacecraft, Mangalyan, has gone into corbit around Mars on the very first try. No other country has ever done this. (2) The spacecraft is in an elliptical orbit, and has a high resolution camera which is taking full-disk colour images of Mars.

'These images will aid planetary scientists,' the NSS observed.

ISRO had on November 5, 2013, launched the Mars Orbiter mission from Sriharikota at a cost of Rs 450 crore, which successfully entered the Martian atmosphere soon after, scripting history of being the first country in the world to have succeeded the mission in its very first attempt.

Answer the following questions in not more than 20 words.

11. When and where was Mangalyan launched?

____

12. What is the name of the US space agency and what is the name of the conferred award?

____

____

13. Briefly mention the two most important achievements of India's Mars Mission.

____

14. Describe the award.

____

____

15. Who would be receiving the award and where?

____

____

____

SPOKEN AND WRITTEN EXPRESSION; PUNCTUATIONS

LEARNING OBJECTIVES

- ➤ Full Stop
- ➤ Exclamation mark
- ➤ Quotation marks
- ➤ Comma
- ➤ Semicolon
- ➤ Hyphens

PRACTICE EXERCISE

Choose the correct punctuation option to make the sentence grammatically correct.

1. Have you seen my shoes
   - (A) Question mark
   - (B) Full stop
   - (C) Exclamation mark
   - (D) Inverted comma

2. Rose said, I don't want to see your face
   - (A) Full stop
   - (B) Question mark
   - (C) Exclamation mark
   - (D) Comma

3. She speaks English Hindi and German
   - (A) Comma
   - (B) Full stop
   - (C) Semi colon
   - (D) Colon

4. The page is divided into three sections the header, the main field and the footer
   - (A) Semi colon
   - (B) Colon
   - (C) Apostrophe
   - (D) Full stop

5. The students answer was brilliant.
   - (A) Semi colon
   - (B) Colon
   - (C) Apostrophe
   - (D) Comma

6. Oh my God – I forgot
   - (A) Apostrophe
   - (B) Full stop
   - (C) Exclamatory mark
   - (D) Inverted comma

7. Why don't you go for medical check-ups
   - (A) Dash
   - (B) Full stop
   - (C) Question Mark
   - (D) Comma

8. I m a student.
   - (A) Full stop
   - (B) Apostrophe
   - (C) Comma
   - (D) Question mark

9. He entered the store and said, I want to buy a new computer
   - (A) Inverted comma
   - (B) Comma
   - (C) Full stop
   - (D) Exclamation mark

10. I have three sisters: Reeta Geeta and Sita
    - (A) Comma
    - (B) Semi colon
    - (C) Apostrophe
    - (D) Exclamation mark

11. What time does the bus arrive
    - (A) Question mark
    - (B) Full stop
    - (C) Comma
    - (D) Exclamation mark

Choose the correct punctuation option to make the sentence grammatically correct.

1. Have you seen my shoes
   (A) Question mark
   (B) Full stop
   (C) Exclamation mark
   (D) Inverted comma

2. Rose said, I don't want to see your face
   (A) Full stop
   (B) Question mark
   (C) Exclamation mark
   (D) Comma

3. She speaks English Hindi and German
   (A) Comma　　　(B) Full stop
   (C) Semi colon　(D) Colon

4. The page is divided into three sections the header, the main field and the footer
   (A) Semi colon　(B) Colon
   (C) Apostrophe　(D) Full stop

5. The students answer was brilliant.
   (A) Semi colon　(B) Colon
   (C) Apostrophe　(D) Comma

6. Oh my God – I forgot
   (A) Apostrophe
   (B) Full stop
   (C) Exclamatory mark
   (D) Inverted comma

7. Why don't you go for medical check-ups
   (A) Dash　　　　(B) Full stop
   (C) Question Mark　(D) Comma

8. I m a student.
   (A) Full stop
   (B) Apostrophe
   (C) Comma
   (D) Question mark

9. He entered the store and said, I want to buy a new computer
   (A) Inverted comma
   (B) Comma
   (C) Full stop
   (D) Exclamation mark

10. I have three sisters: Reeta Geeta and Sita
    (A) Comma
    (B) Semi colon
    (C) Apostrophe
    (D) Exclamation mark

11. What time does the bus arrive
    (A) Question mark
    (B) Full stop
    (C) Comma
    (D) Exclamatory mark

12. What is your favourite season
    (A) Comma
    (B) Full stop
    (C) Question mark
    (D) Exclamatory mark

13. My brother plays football
    (A) Comma
    (B) Full stop
    (C) Question mark
    (D) Exclamatory mark

14. I love to read good books
    (A) Question mark
    (B) Full stop
    (C) Comma
    (D) Exclamatory mark

15. In five minutes the shop will be closed.
    (A) Question mark
    (B) Full stop
    (C) Comma
    (D) Exclamatory mark

16. When I get home I go and brush my teeth.
    (A) Question mark
    (B) Full stop
    (C) Comma
    (D) Exclamatory mark

17. Until I reach my goal I won't stop working.
    (A) Question mark
    (B) Comma
    (C) Full stop
    (D) Exclamatory mark

18. This is Mr Ravis house
    (A) Comma   (B) Apostrophe
    (C) Full stop   (D) Question mark
19. Please close the door of the car
    (A) Comma   (B) Apostrophe
    (C) Full stop   (D) Question mark

20. Do you want to walk to the river side
    (A) Comma
    (B) Apostrophe
    (C) Full stop
    (D) Question mark

HOTS (ACHIEVERS SECTION)

21. Select the correct option from the sentences given below.
    (A) "The magician explained, "I will pull a rabbit out of this hat."
    (B) "The magician explained I will pull a rabbit out of this hat."
    (C) The magician explained I will pull a "rabbit" out of this "hat."
    (D) "The magician explained I will pull out a rabbit out of this hat."

22. Select the correct option from the sentences given below.
    (A) That was an exciting trick. Exclaimed Margaret.
    (B) "That was an exciting trick!" exclaimed Margaret.
    (C) That was an exciting trick, exclaimed Margaret.
    (D) "That was an exciting trick! exclaimed Margaret.

23. Directions: Put the comma in the sentences given below. Well can you do it for me now?
    (A) Well, can you do it for me now?
    (B) Well can you do it, for me now?
    (C) Well can you do it for me, now?
    (D) Well can you do it for me now?

24. Directions: Put the comma in the sentences given below. Yes my party is tomorrow after school.
    (A) Yes, my party is tomorrow after school.
    (B) Yes my party, is tomorrow after school.
    (C) Yes my party is tomorrow, after school.
    (D) Yes my party is tomorrow after, school.

25. Directions: Put the comma in the sentences given below.
    Dereck John David and Paul are in the same team.
    (A) Dereck, John David and Paul are in the same team.
    (B) Dereck John David, and Paul are in the same team.
    (C) Dereck, John. David, and Paul, are in the same team.
    (D) Dereck, John, David and Paul are in the same team.

—Darken Your Choice with HB Pencil—

	A B C D		A B C D		A B C D		A B C D		A B C D
1.	Ⓐ Ⓑ Ⓒ Ⓓ	6.	Ⓐ Ⓑ Ⓒ Ⓓ	11.	Ⓐ Ⓑ Ⓒ Ⓓ	16	Ⓐ Ⓑ Ⓒ Ⓓ	21.	Ⓐ Ⓑ Ⓒ Ⓓ
2.	Ⓐ Ⓑ Ⓒ Ⓓ	7.	Ⓐ Ⓑ Ⓒ Ⓓ	12.	Ⓐ Ⓑ Ⓒ Ⓓ	17.	Ⓐ Ⓑ Ⓒ Ⓓ	22.	Ⓐ Ⓑ Ⓒ Ⓓ
3.	Ⓐ Ⓑ Ⓒ Ⓓ	8.	Ⓐ Ⓑ Ⓒ Ⓓ	13.	Ⓐ Ⓑ Ⓒ Ⓓ	18.	Ⓐ Ⓑ Ⓒ Ⓓ	23.	Ⓐ Ⓑ Ⓒ Ⓓ
4.	Ⓐ Ⓑ Ⓒ Ⓓ	9.	Ⓐ Ⓑ Ⓒ Ⓓ	14.	Ⓐ Ⓑ Ⓒ Ⓓ	19.	Ⓐ Ⓑ Ⓒ Ⓓ	24.	Ⓐ Ⓑ Ⓒ Ⓓ
5.	Ⓐ Ⓑ Ⓒ Ⓓ	10.	Ⓐ Ⓑ Ⓒ Ⓓ	15.	Ⓐ Ⓑ Ⓒ Ⓓ	20.	Ⓐ Ⓑ Ⓒ Ⓓ	25.	Ⓐ Ⓑ Ⓒ Ⓓ

MODEL TEST PAPER

SECTION I : Word And Structure Knowledge

Direction (1–5): Complete the idioms by choosing the correct options.

1. __________sword
   (A) Broken   (B) Long
   (C) Fencing   (D) Double-edged

2. A picture paints a ______________
   (A) thousand words (B) moment
   (C) scene   (D) feeling

3. Big ________ in a __________ pond.
   (A) duck, happy   (B) tuna, dirty
   (C) fish, small   (D) frog, green

4. Necessity is the mother of ________.
   (A) need   (B) invention
   (C) children   (D) depression

5. Fair weather makes __________
   (A) friends   (B) buddies
   (C) enemies   (D) uncles

Direction (6–10): Choose the correct word options to fill in the blanks.

6. There was______much food to eat at the party.
   (A) too   (B) to
   (C) for   (D) none

7. I couldn't ______ to leave my puppy at home.
   (A) bare   (B) bear
   (C) bore   (D) none

8. ______phones had been confiscated for two weeks.
   (A) His   (B) There
   (C) Their   (D) None

9. I made a ______with my best friend to never forget her.
   (A) pact   (B) packed
   (C) sign   (D) none

10. Preeta has such a tiny __________.
    (A) wast   (B) waist
    (C) wast   (D) none

Directions (11–15): Find out the correct options to punctuate the following sentences properly.

11. He woke up late so he had to drive to work
    (A) Full stop
    (B) Comma
    (C) Question mark
    (D) Inverted commas

12. I don't like horror films
    (A) Question mark
    (B) Comma
    (C) Full stop
    (D) Exclamatory mark

13. How do you like this city
    (A) Comma
    (B) Question mark
    (C) Full stop
    (D) None of these

14. They re on their way home from the party
    (A) Apostrophe
    (B) Question mark
    (C) Full stop
    (D) None of these

15. I don't feel well, said Suzy
    (A) Comma
    (B) Question mark
    (C) Inverted commas
    (D) Apostrophe

Directions (16–20): Fill in the blanks with the correct prepositions.

16. The dog ran _______ the traffic jam.
    (A) on   (B) into
    (C) through   (D) at
17. He jumped _____ the fence.
    (A) at   (B) over
    (C) above   (D) on
18. I fell asleep _____ the shade.
    (A) below   (B) in
    (C) above   (D) under
19. You should stay away ____ bad people.
    (A) from   (B) to
    (C) upon   (D) into
20. Take pride ___ doing a good deed.
    (A) on   (B) at
    (C) in   (D) up

SECTION II: Reading

Since 1993 World Water Day is celebrated on March 22. It was declared as such by the United Nations General Assembly. This day was first formally proposed in Agenda 21 of the 1992 United Nations Conference on Environment and Development (UNCED) in Rio de Janeiro, Brazil. It began in 1993 and has grown to be significant ever since.

The UN and its member nations devote this day to implementing UN recommendations and promoting concrete activities within their countries regarding the world's water resources. Each year, one of the various UN agencies involved in water issues takes the lead in promoting and coordinating international activities for World Water Day.

In addition to the UN member states, a number of NGOs promoting clean water and sustainable aquatic habitats have used World Day for Water as a time to focus public attention on the critical water issues of our era. Every three years since 1997, for instance, the World Water Council has drawn thousands to participate in its World Water Forum during the week of World Day for Water. Participating agencies and NGOs have highlighted issues such as a billion people being without access to safe drinking water and the role of gender in a family's access to safe water.

Answer these questions on the basis of the information given in the above paragraph.

21. World Water Day is held on March 22, 1992.
    (A) True   (B) False
    (C) None of these
22. Only UN member states are involved with the promotion of World Water Day.
    (A) True   (B) False
    (C) None of these
23. What does 'Aquatic' pertain to?
    (A) Air   (B) Animals
    (C) Earth   (D) Water
24. Not everybody has access to drinking water.
    (A) True   (B) False
    (C) None of these
25. Where is Rio de Janeiro?
    (A) America   (B) Australia
    (C) Brazil   (D) Canada

Look at the picture below and answer the questions that follow.

26. What happened to the village?
    (A) There was a landslide
    (B) There was a fire
    (C) It was barren
    (D) It got flooded

27. Who are the men in the picture?
   (A) Rescuemen
   (B) Firemen
   (C) Policemen
   (D) Soldiers
28. What happened to the child?
   (A) She wanted her pet dog
   (B) She lost her favourite shoe
   (C) She got separated from her family
   (D) She had fever
29. What is such an event called?
   (A) An unhappy occurrence
   (B) A party
   (C) Natural disaster
   (D) A tornado
30. What is it called when people are trying to manage such a situation?
   (A) Natural happenstance
   (B) Nature management
   (C) Disaster coordination
   (D) Disaster management

SECTION III: Spoken And Written Section
Directions(31–33): Choose the correct option and fill in the blanks.

31. John welcomed his guests _______ offered them drinks.
   (A) and   (B) but
   (C) so   (D) that
32. _______ he is thin, he is strong.
   (A) Over
   (B) On
   (C) Though
   (D) Above
33. These rooms are very comfortable _______ they have a good view of the city.
   (A) at
   (B) on
   (C) as
   (D) over
34. Tony: Hey, where are you going?
   Mick:
   (A) It's a secret
   (B) To my friend's house.
   (C) Why do you care ?
   (D) Not your business
35. Minnie: I'm feeling sad.
   Jack:
   (A) Who cares?
   (B) So am I !
   (C) Why? What happened?
   (D) Even my life is hard.

Darken Your Choice with HB Pencil

	A B C D		A B C D		A B C D		A B C D		A B C D
1.	Ⓐ Ⓑ Ⓒ Ⓓ	8.	Ⓐ Ⓑ Ⓒ Ⓓ	15.	Ⓐ Ⓑ Ⓒ Ⓓ	22.	Ⓐ Ⓑ Ⓒ Ⓓ	29.	Ⓐ Ⓑ Ⓒ Ⓓ
2.	Ⓐ Ⓑ Ⓒ Ⓓ	9.	Ⓐ Ⓑ Ⓒ Ⓓ	16.	Ⓐ Ⓑ Ⓒ Ⓓ	23.	Ⓐ Ⓑ Ⓒ Ⓓ	30.	Ⓐ Ⓑ Ⓒ Ⓓ
3.	Ⓐ Ⓑ Ⓒ Ⓓ	10.	Ⓐ Ⓑ Ⓒ Ⓓ	17.	Ⓐ Ⓑ Ⓒ Ⓓ	24.	Ⓐ Ⓑ Ⓒ Ⓓ	31.	Ⓐ Ⓑ Ⓒ Ⓓ
4.	Ⓐ Ⓑ Ⓒ Ⓓ	11.	Ⓐ Ⓑ Ⓒ Ⓓ	18.	Ⓐ Ⓑ Ⓒ Ⓓ	25.	Ⓐ Ⓑ Ⓒ Ⓓ	32.	Ⓐ Ⓑ Ⓒ Ⓓ
5.	Ⓐ Ⓑ Ⓒ Ⓓ	12.	Ⓐ Ⓑ Ⓒ Ⓓ	19.	Ⓐ Ⓑ Ⓒ Ⓓ	26.	Ⓐ Ⓑ Ⓒ Ⓓ	33.	Ⓐ Ⓑ Ⓒ Ⓓ
6.	Ⓐ Ⓑ Ⓒ Ⓓ	13.	Ⓐ Ⓑ Ⓒ Ⓓ	20.	Ⓐ Ⓑ Ⓒ Ⓓ	27.	Ⓐ Ⓑ Ⓒ Ⓓ	34.	Ⓐ Ⓑ Ⓒ Ⓓ
7.	Ⓐ Ⓑ Ⓒ Ⓓ	14.	Ⓐ Ⓑ Ⓒ Ⓓ	21.	Ⓐ Ⓑ Ⓒ Ⓓ	28.	Ⓐ Ⓑ Ⓒ Ⓓ	35.	Ⓐ Ⓑ Ⓒ Ⓓ

HINTS AND SOLUTIONS

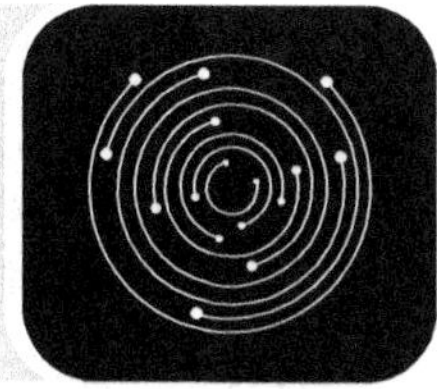

1. WORD POWER

Answer Key

1. (C)	2. (B)	3. (D)	4. (A)	5. (D)	6. (A)	7. (B)	8. (B)	9. (A)	10. (C)
11. Roadways	12. Airways	13. Railways		14. Railways		15. Railways
16. Roadways	17. Railways	18. Airways		19 Waterways		20. Airways
21. Hostile	22. Carelessness	23. Reasonable		24. Trustworthy		25. Bravery

HOTS (ACHIEVERS SECTION)

26. (C)	27. (C)	28. (A)	29. (A)	30. (C)

2. SYNONYMS AND ANTONYMS

Answer Key

1. (C)	2. (C)	3. (D)	4. (C)	5. (B)	6. (C)	7. (C)	8. (C)	9. (D)	10. (D)
11. (C)	12. (D)	13. (C)	14. (C)	15. (D)	16. (D)	17. (D)	18. (C)	19. (A)	20. (D)
21. (D)	22. (D)	23. (A)	24. (D)	25. (D)					

HOTS (ACHIEVERS SECTION)

26. (D)	27. (D)	28. (D)	29. (D)	30. (A)

3. HOMONYMS AND HOMOPHONES

Answer Key

1. (B)	2. (A)	3. (B)	4. (A)	5. (D)	6. (B)	7. (A)	8. (A)	9. (B)	10. (A)
11. (B)	12. (A)	13. (B)	14. (B)	15. (B)	16. (B)	17. (B)	18. (B)	19. (B)	20. (B)
21. There	22. To; too	23. Write	24. Ate, whole		25. Pane				

HOTS (ACHIEVERS SECTION)

26. (B)	27. (C)	28. (A)	29. (D)	30. (C)

4. COLLOCATION AND IDIOMS

Answer Key

1. (C)	2. (D)	3. (B)	4. (A)	5. (C)	6. (A)	7. (B)	8. (C)	9. (B)	10. (C)
11. (D)	12. (B)	13. (A)	14. (B)	15. (A)	16. (B)	17. (A)	18. (C)	19. (A)	20. (D)
21. (D)	22. (D)	23. (B)	24. (C)	25. (D)					

HOTS (ACHIEVERS SECTION)

26. (C)	27. (D)	28. (D)	29. (C)	30. (B)

5. NOUN

Answer Key

1. (D)	2. (C)	3. (C)	4. (C)	5. (D)	6. (D)	7. (D)	8. (B)	9. (B)	10. (C)
11. (C)	12. (B)	13. (B)	14. (B)	15. (B)					

HOTS (ACHIEVERS SECTION)

1. We saw a shoal of fish swimming in the lake.
   Shoal – Collective Noun.
   Lake – Common Noun.

2. My brother plays the piano very well.
   Brother – Common Noun.
   Piano – Common Noun.

3. She put her bag on the table.
   Bag – Common Noun.
   Table – Common Noun.

4. Ganga is a holy river.
   Ganga – Proper Noun.
   River – Common Noun.

5. India is the seventh-largest country in the world.
   India – Proper Noun.
   Country – Common Noun.
   World – Common Noun.

6. PRONOUN

Answer Key

1. (B)	2. (D)	3. (B)	4. (D)	5. (A)	6. (D)	7. (A)	8. (D)	9. (B)	10. (C)
11. Who	12. That	13. That	14. Which	15. Whose	16. Whose	17. Where	18. Where	19. Whose	20. Whom
21. (D)	22. (A)	23. (C)	24. (B)	25. (E)					

HOTS (ACHIEVERS SECTION)

Subject Pronoun	Object Pronoun	Possessive Pronoun	Reflexive pronoun
1. they	them	theirs	Themselves
2. she	her	hers	Herself
3. he	him	his	Himself
4. you	your	yours	Yourself, yourselves
5. we	us	ours	Ourselves

7. VERBS AND ADVERBS

Answer Key

1. Stole	2. Went	3. Felt	4. Went	5. Went
6. Ate	7. Bought	8. Thought	9. Ate	10. Met
11. (B)	12. (A)	13. (D)	14. (A)	15. (C)
16. (A)	17. (D)	18. (A)	19. (C)	20. (B)
21. (A)	22. (C)	23. (C)	24. (A)	25. (C)

HOTS (ACHIEVERS SECTION)

26. SWAM → SWUM	27. WROTE → WRITTEN	28. (B)	29. (B)	30. (D)

1. (B) Adverbs are the words that modify verbs, adjectives and other adverbs, whereas adjectives are words that modify nouns and pronouns.

2. (B) Adverbs can modify the adjectives but not vice versa. The position of adverbs in relation to verbs can vary. Examples: I disagree with you completely. I completely disagree with you. I disagree completely with you.

3. (D) "Usually" in these sentences is an adverb of manner. In both A and B its position is correct.

8. ADJECTIVES

Answer Key

1. (A)	2. (B)	3. (D)	4. (C)	5. (D)	6. (C)	7. (D)	8. (D)	9. (C)	10. (A)
11. (D)	12. (D)	13. (A)	14. (A)	15. (D)	16. (A)	17. (A)	18. (A)	19. (C)	20. (C)

HOTS (ACHIEVERS SECTION)

1. (D)	2. (A)	3. (B)	4. (D)	5. (D)

1. (D) Correction for incorrect options: B. Do you have any further plans for adding on to the building? D. That's a lot farther than I want to carry this heavy suitcase!

2. (A) Correction for incorrect options: B. Of the first two Harry Potter books, I prefer the latter. C. John arrived at the party later than Mary did.

3. (B) Correction for incorrect options: A. I have less than an hour to do this work. C. People these days are buying fewer newspapers.

4. (D) Correction for the options: A. Out of chapters 1, 2 and 3, the last one is the most difficult to learn B. Dan is now friends with Ruth, Maya and Ben. The latter is his cousin.

9. ARTICLES

Answer Key

1. (C)	2. (B)	3. (B)	4. (B)	5. (C)	6. (B)	7. (B)	8. (B)	9. (C)	10. (C)
11. (D)	12. (B)	13. (C)	14. (A)	15. (C)	16. (C)	17. (A)	18. (A)	19. (A)	20. (C)

HOTS (ACHIEVERS SECTION)

21. (D)	22. (B)	23. (D)	24. (B)	25. (D)

1. (D) Articles are used before nouns or noun equivalents and are a type of adjective. The definite article (the) is used before a noun to indicate that the identity of the noun is known to the reader or the noun is specific. The indefinite article (a, an) is used before a noun that is general or when its identity is not known. 'The' is used with both singular and plural noun while 'a/an' is used with singular noun.

'children', 'honour' and 'Prime Minister' are specific noun and 'the' preposition is used whereas 'poem' is general word because there are many poems any specific name is not taken hence 'a' is used.

2. (B) Articles are used before nouns or noun equivalents and are a type of adjective. The definite article (the) is used before a noun to indicate that the identity of the noun is known to the reader or the noun is specific. The indefinite article (a, an) is used before a noun that is general or when its identity is not known. 'The' is used with both singular and plural noun while 'a/an' is used with singular noun.

In the sentence 'fish' is general noun and 'bottle' is specific noun. Hence 'a' before fish and 'the' before 'bottle' is used.

3. (D) Articles are used before nouns or noun equivalents and are a type of adjective. The definite article (the) is used before a noun to indicate that the identity of the noun is known to the reader or the noun is specific. The indefinite article (a, an) is used before a noun that is general or when its identity is not known. 'The' is used with both singular and plural noun while 'a/an' is used with singular noun.

In the sentence 'good deal' is indefinite but 'war' is specific. Hence, 'a' before 'good deal' and 'the' before 'war'.

4. **(B)** 'The' is used before specific things/places. No article is used before proper nouns. Here, platform is specific - it is the wrong one. Platform 3 and platform 8 are proper nouns.

5. **(D)** For indefinite, uncountable nouns, either no article is used, or we use a word that describes quantity such as some, considerable, little. Hence, no article before 'wisdom'. 'Great' is used in general sense and therefore 'a' article is used.

10. PREPOSITIONS

Answer Key

1. (C)	2. (B)	3. (D)	4. (A)	5. (D)	6. (A)	7. (B)	8. (B)	9. (A)	10. (C)
11. Between		12. But		13. Under		14. Before		15. For	
16. Among		17. Along		18. Of		19 Into		20. Above	
21. Off		22. Over		23. To		24. Through		25. Towards	

HOTS (ACHIEVERS SECTION)

26. With	27. In	28. To	29. By	30. Through

1. **(B)** Adverbs are the words that modify verbs, adjectives and other adverbs, whereas adjectives are words that modify nouns and pronouns.

2. **(B)** Adverbs can modify the adjectives but not vice versa. The position of adverbs in relation to verbs can vary. Examples: I disagree with you completely. I completely disagree with you. I disagree completely with you.

3. **(D)** "Usually" in these sentences is an adverb of manner. In both A and B its position is correct.

4. **(D)** Unlike other summers, we will seldom go out because mom will give birth to my baby brother. Here 'seldom' is the adverb of manner.

5. **(A)** Summer vacation is coming soon. Here 'soon' is the adverb of time.

11. CONJUNCTIONS

Answer Key

1. (A)	2. (C)	3. (A)	4. (B)	5. (B)	6. (C)	7. (B)	8. (A)	9. (C)	10. (A)
11. (A)	12. (A)	13. (A)	14. (B)	15. (A)	16. (B)	17. (D)	18. (B)	19. (C)	20. (B)

1. **(A)**
Option (A) is correct because meaning of meticulousness means precise, brief which is synonym of precision. Other options are having different meaning which are not synonym of precise.

2. **(C)**
'Such as' is used to provide specific examples of something you are talking about. Here in the sentence, New York or London are the specific examples. 'Such' is followed by 'as' in the sentence when specific examples are given. Thus, according to the rules of usage, option (C) is the correct answer. Rest of the options are incorrect.

3. **(A)**
The concept of conjunctions is required to determine the correct answer in the given sentence. So-that is a subordinating conjunction that connects the main and the independent clause to express the cause or reason.
Option (A) is used to suggest a contrast. Thus option (A) is incorrect.
Option (C), then, indicates time. Thus option (C) is incorrect.
Option (D), so, is incorrect as so-so is not a correct subordinating conjunction and cannot be used to link the clauses.
Thus option (B), that, is the correct answer.

4. **(B)**
Arvind says he does not like the trainer but he likes the decor.
There is a contrast in opinions as he likes one thing and doesn't like another. When we have to show such contrast, we usually use the conjunction 'but'.
So, the correct answer is (B).

5. **(B)**
Conjunctions are words that link other words, phrases, or clauses together. The structure no sooner is used to talk about something that happens immediately after something else. When no sooner comes at the beginning of a sentence, we use inverted word order. That means the auxiliary verb comes before the subject.

The conjunction 'No sooner ---- than' is also used to denote simultaneous actions. The given sentence depicts that as soon as I received her text, I left for her house immediately. These two activities take place almost simultaneously. There is no real time difference between them. Thus Option B is correct. Option A can be ruled out as but is used to introduce a word or phrase that contrasts with what was said before. 'For' explains reason or sights purpose. Thus Option D can be ruled out. We can use 'when' to introduce a single completed event that takes place in the middle of a longer activity or event. In these cases, we usually use a continuous verb in the main clause to describe the background event. Thus Option C is incorrect as it cannot be used along with 'no sooner'.

6. **(C)**
A conjunction combines or connects two sentences as one. They can either be a word or a phrase (like even if, as well as, etc). Correlative conjunctions are words in pairs that connect two sentences, but they're not written together, for example, either...or, but...and, such...that etc. where there's a word/s in between the pair. 'So that' and 'so...that' have different meanings. 'So that' refers to purpose, it expresses the reason for which an action is carried out, as in 'I left early so that I could attend the party'. The given sentence does not focus on purpose, but the result, where 'so' emphasizes a quality or condition, here it emphasizes "ill", and "that" brings out the result "doctors suspect he may not survive". This can be seen in option C, which is correct. In option A, 'so that' refers to purpose, it sounds as if the purpose for Mike being ill was that the doctors suspect he might not survive, which sounds illogical, hence option A is incorrect. In B, the sentence sounds a little off, because 'that' has been placed between the result, but the result should include the doctors' suspecting, 'that' should be placed right

after "ill", as it refers to the effect that follows, hence option B is incorrect. In option D, the correlatives 'so...that' have been interchanged in order, 'that' has been used in place of 'so' and vice versa. The sentence does not have a proper meaning, 'that' in this sentence acts as a demonstrative, and the order isn't correct, hence option D is incorrect.

7. **(B)**

A conjunction combines or connects two sentences as one. They can be a word or a phrase (like even if, as well as, etc). Correlative conjunctions are words in pairs that connect two sentences, but they're not written together, for example, either...or, but...and, such...that etc, where there's a word or phrase in between the pair. 'So that' and 'so...that' have different meanings. 'So that' refers to purpose, it expresses the reason for which an action is carried out, as in 'I left early so that I could attend the party'. The given sentence does not focus on purpose, but the result, his being tall prevented him from fitting in the car, the position of 'so...that' determines the meaning of the sentence. 'So' is placed before 'tall' to express the result "not fit in the car" of being "tall". The option with the correct sentence is Option B, as it has the required placement of 'so' and 'that'. They should not be placed together, as in options A and C, in A, the sentence expresses the purpose of being tall, so he does not fit in the car, but it's incorrect in terms of grammar as well as logic. In C, the sentence is grammatically incorrect, emphasizing on the action of his being "He is", hence these are both incorrect. Sentences that begin with 'so' refer to a cause and are usually a continuation of the previous sentence, as in 'She couldn't take the stress anymore. So, she left her job'. The sentence here does not focus on the cause, but the effect or result. Hence option D is incorrect.

8. **(A)**

A conjunction combines or connects two sentences as one. They can be a word or a phrase (like even if, as well as, etc). Correlative conjunctions are words in pairs that connect two sentences, but they're not written together, for example, either...or, but...and, such...that etc, where a word or a phrase is in between the pair (either rice or noodles). 'So that' and 'so...that' have different meanings. 'So that' refers to purpose, it expresses the reason for which an action is carried out, as in 'I left early so that I could attend the party'. 'So...that' refers to a situation of cause and result. The given sentence does not focus on purpose, but the result, where 'so' functions as an intensifier for the adjective "short" and 'that' refers to the result of David being short "he can't reach the top of the shelf". This can be seen in Option A, hence it's correct. In option B, 'so that' has been used, it refers to purpose, and changes the meaning of the sentence to 'the purpose of David being short is that he cannot reach the top of the shelf'. It does not mean the same as the given sentences, hence option B is incorrect. In option C, the order of 'so...that' has been altered, where 'that' replaces 'so', it acts as a demonstrative of 'short', it does not refer to the result as it's supposed to. Instead, 'so' refers to the result by making it sound like a cause, 'so' on its own refers to a reason or cause, hence option C is incorrect. In option D, 'so that' refers to purpose and not result, it refers to "David is short" as the purpose. But, we don't need to use 'so that', but 'so...that', which are different in meaning. Hence option D is incorrect.

9. **(C)**

A conjunction combines or connects two sentences as one. They can be a word or a phrase (like even if, as well as, etc). Correlative conjunctions are words in pairs that connect two sentences, but they're not written together, for example, either...or, but...and, such...that etc, where a word or a phrase is in between the pair (either rice or noodles). 'So that' and 'so...that' have different meanings. 'So that' refers to purpose, it expresses the reason for which an action is carried out, as in 'I left early so that I could attend the party'. The given sentences do not focus on purpose, but the result, 'so' intensifies the adjective "steep" and 'that' refers to the result of the hill being steep "we couldn't climb to the top". This can be seen in option C, hence it's correct. In option A, the error is in "So steep the hill was", sentences with 'so... that' do not begin with 'so', and the formation of this part is not right, hence A is incorrect. In B, the sentence contains 'so that', which refers to purpose, the meaning of the sentence changes to 'the hill became steep for the purpose that we could not climb it', which is not what the original sentences meant, hence option B is incorrect. In D, the order of 'so...that' has been altered, instead of referring to the result, 'that' demonstrates the cause and result as a whole. As the order of 'so...that' has been altered, option D is incorrect.

10. (A)
A conjunction combines or connects two sentences or words together. In the given sentence, the clause "he could practice for the audition" is the subordinate/ dependent clause as it depends on the main/independent clause "He left the show" for its full meaning. A conjunction can be a word, or a phrase as the one here, "so...", we need to find the correct word from these options to complete the phrase. The subordinate clause is the purpose or reason behind which the action in the main clause "left the show" takes place. 'That' is a conjunction used in purpose related sentences, and when paired with 'so', it expresses purpose, hence option A is correct. 'Then' is an adverb that relates to time, meaning 'immediately', but we require a conjunction here, hence option B is incorrect. 'As' is a conjunction that refers to cause-related sentences. There is a minor difference between cause and purpose. Purpose is the reason for which something is done or created, whereas cause is the justification or explanation for an action carried out. This sentence is purpose-related, hence option C is incorrect. Similarly, 'because' is cause-related, hence option D is also incorrect.

11. (A)
'So that' is used to talk about a purpose. In the given sentence, the purpose is buying the earrings. 'So' is followed by an adjective. Options B, C and D are grammatically wrong. Thus, option A is the correct answer.

12. (A)
A conjunction combines or connects two sentences as one. They can be a word or a phrase (like even if, as well as, etc). Correlative conjunctions are words in pairs that connect two sentences, but they're not written together, for example, either...or, but...and, such... that etc, where a word or phrase is in between the pair, (either rice or noodles). 'So that' and 'so...that' have different meanings. 'So that' refers to purpose, it expresses the reason for which an action is carried out, as in 'I left early so that I could attend the party'. The given sentence does not focus on purpose, but the result, 'so' emphasizes the quality of being arrogant, which results in "he would never ask for help". This can be seen in option A, hence it's correct. 'So that' in option B refers to a purpose, the sentence changes the meaning to 'for the purpose of not asking for help, James is arrogant', which isn't true, hence option B is incorrect. The construction of 'So arrogant James is' is incorrect, as a sentence of this type cannot begin with 'so', hence C is incorrect. 'That' in D functions as a demonstrative adjective, referring to James, whereas 'so...that' is supposed to focus on the effect of being arrogant. The order has also changed, where 'that' precedes 'so', making option D incorrect for these reasons.

13. (A)

A conjunction combines or connects two sentences as one. They can be a word or a phrase (like even if, as well as, etc). Correlative conjunctions are words in pairs that connect two sentences, but they're not written together, for example, either...or, but...and, such...that etc, where a word or a phrase is in between the pair (either rice or noodles). 'So that' and 'so...that' have different meanings. 'So that' refers to purpose, it expresses the reason for which an action is carried out, as in 'I left early so that I could attend the party'. The given sentence does not focus on purpose, but the result, 'so' intensifies the adjective "cold" and 'that' refers to the result of being cold "we couldn't play outdoors", this can be seen in A, hence option A is correct. In options B and C, 'so that' refers to purpose, and changes the meaning of the sentence, in B it means 'it became cold to prevent the people from playing outdoors'. The sentence in C means 'not being able to play outdoors for the purpose to make it cold'. These sentences don't focus on the cause and result, like in the original pair of sentences, hence options B and C are incorrect. Similarly, the sentence in D has also changed in meaning, where 'that' modifies the clause containing 'so', "it was so cold", which isn't the correct order, 'that' should precede the result "we couldn't play outdoors", hence D is also incorrect.

14. (B)

A conjunction combines or connects two sentences as one. They can be a word or a phrase (like even if, as well as, etc). Correlative conjunctions are words in pairs that connect two sentences, but they're not written together, for example, either...or, but...and, such...that etc, where a word or a phrase is in between the pair (either rice or noodles). 'So that' and 'so...that' have different meanings. 'So that' refers to purpose, it expresses

the reason for which an action is carried out, as in 'I left early so that I could attend the party'. The given sentence does not focus on purpose, but the result, where 'so' refers to the adjective 'bright' and 'that' refers to the result of it being bright "it hurt my eyes", this can be seen in B, hence option B is correct. In option A, 'so that' focuses on purpose, and changes the meaning of the sentence to 'it was bright for the reason that it could hurt my eyes', which isn't what the original sentence means, hence A is incorrect. In option C, the order of 'so...that' has been altered, where 'that' refers to the adjective 'bright' and functions as a demonstrative, but in the construction 'so...that', it's supposed to refer to the result, hence option C is incorrect. In option D, 'so bright it was' is incorrect in terms of order, where the adjective 'bright' precedes the subject 'it'. Sentences with 'so...that' do not begin with 'so', hence option D is incorrect.

15. (A)

Correlative Conjunction is always used in pairs and denote equality, and show the relationship between ideas expressed in different parts of a sentence - and thus make the joining tighter and more emphatic. Some examples are either/or, neither/nor, and not only/but also. The structure no sooner is used to talk about something that happens immediately after something else. It is often used with the past perfect, and usually followed by than. In the given sentence it is inferred that she finished reading his letter and immediately fainted. These two activities take place almost simultaneously. There is no real time difference between them. Thus Option A is correct. We can use 'when' to introduce a single completed event that takes place in the middle of a longer activity or event. In these cases, we usually use a continuous verb in the main clause to describe the background event. Thus Option D is incorrect as it cannot be used along with 'no sooner'. Option B can be ruled out as the conjunction 'but' is used to suggest a contrast. After shows "subsequently to the time when". Thus Option C can be discarded as it is clearly mentioned in the sentence that two activities take place almost simultaneously.

16. **(B)**
Correlative Conjunction is always used in pairs and denote equality, and show the relationship between ideas expressed in different parts of a sentence - and thus make the joining tighter and more emphatic. Some examples are either/or, neither/nor, and not only/but also. The structure no sooner is used to talk about something that happens immediately after something else. It is often used with the past perfect, and usually followed by than. In the given sentence it is inferred that she finished her task and immediately went to the next one. These two activities take place almost simultaneously. There is no real time difference between them. Thus Option B is correct. We can use 'when' to introduce a single completed event that takes place in the middle of a longer activity or event. In these cases, we usually use a continuous verb in the main clause to describe the background event. Thus Option C is incorrect as it cannot be used along with 'no sooner'. Option A can be ruled out as the conjunction 'but' is used to suggest a contrast. After shows "subsequently to the time when". Thus Option D can be discarded as it is clearly mentioned that two activities take place almost simultaneously.

17. **(D)**
Conjunctions are words that link other words, phrases, or clauses together.
The structure no sooner is used to talk about something that happens immediately after something else. When no sooner comes at the beginning of a sentence, we use inverted word order. That means the auxiliary verb comes before the subject. The conjunction

'No sooner ---- than' is also used to denote simultaneous actions. The given sentence depicts that as soon as the child started crying, his father lifted him up immediately. These two activities take place almost simultaneously. There is no real time difference between them. Thus Option D is correct. Option A can be ruled out as 'Then' indicates 'in that case'. We use 'then' with 'if' to talk about cause and effect but it cannot be used in association with 'no sooner' which is used in case of an event happening immediately after something else. 'After' shows "subsequently to the time when". Thus Option C can be discarded as it is clearly mentioned that two activities take place almost simultaneously. 'Option B can be ruled out as the conjunction 'but' is used to suggest a contrast.

18. **(B)**
Correlative Conjunction is always used in pairs and denote equality, and show the relationship between ideas expressed in different parts of a sentence - and thus make the joining tighter and more emphatic. Some examples are either/or, neither/nor, and not only/but also. The structure no sooner is used to talk about something that happens immediately after something else. It is often used with the past perfect, and usually followed by than. In the given sentence it is inferred that she finished her task and immediately went to the next one. These two activities take place almost simultaneously. There is no real time difference between them. Thus Option B is correct. We can use 'when' to introduce a single completed event that takes place in the middle of a longer activity or event. In these cases, we usually use a continuous verb in the main clause to describe the background event. Thus Option C is incorrect as it cannot be used along with 'no sooner'. Option A can be ruled out as the conjunction 'but' is used to suggest a contrast. After shows "subsequently to the time when". Thus

Option D can be discarded as it is clearly mentioned that two activities take place almost simultaneously.

19. **(C)**
Correlative Conjunction is always used in pairs and denote equality, and show the relationship between ideas expressed in different parts of a sentence - and thus make the joining tighter and more emphatic. Some examples are either/or, neither/nor, and not only/but also. The structure no sooner is used to talk about something that happens immediately after something else. It is often used with the past perfect, and usually followed by than. In the given sentence it is inferred that they finished their work and immediately asked for their salaries. These two activities take place almost simultaneously. There is no real time difference between them. Thus option C is correct. We can use 'when' to introduce a single completed event that takes place in the middle of a longer activity or event. In these cases, we usually use a continuous verb in the main clause to describe the background event. Thus option D is incorrect as it cannot be used along with 'no sooner'. The conjunction 'but' is used to suggest a contrast but it cannot be used along with 'no sooner than'. Thus Option B can be ruled out. For explains reason or sights purpose. Thus Option A is discarded.

20. **(B)**
Correlative Conjunction is always used in pairs and denote equality, and show the relationship between ideas expressed in different parts of a sentence - and thus make the joining tighter and more emphatic. Some examples are either/or, neither/nor, and not only/but also. The structure no sooner is used to talk about something that happens immediately after something else. It is often used with the past perfect, and usually followed by than. In the given sentence it is inferred that I took a dose of aspirin and immediately I started feeling better. These two activities take place almost simultaneously. There is no real time difference between them. Thus Option B is correct. We can use 'when' to introduce a single completed event that takes place in the middle of a longer activity or event. In these cases, we usually use a continuous verb in the main clause to describe the background event. Thus Option D is incorrect as it cannot be used along with 'no sooner'. After shows "subsequently to the time when". Thus Option A can be discarded as it is clearly mentioned in the sentence that two activities take place almost simultaneously. Option C can be ruled out as 'Then' indicates 'in that case'. We use 'then' with 'if' to talk about cause and effect but it cannot be used in association with 'no sooner' which is used in case of an event happening immediately after something else.

HOTS (ACHIEVERS SECTION)

21. (A)	22. (B)	23. (C)	24. (A)	25. (D)

1. **(A)**
Correlative Conjunction is always used in pairs and denote equality, and show the relationship between ideas expressed in different parts of a sentence - and thus make the joining tighter and more emphatic. Some examples are either/or, neither/nor, and not only/but also. The structure no sooner is used to talk about something that happens immediately after something else. It is often used with the past perfect, and usually followed by than. In the given sentence it is inferred that he reaches the train station and immediately the train arrived. These two activities take

place almost simultaneously. There is no real time difference between them. Thus Option A is correct. Option D can be ruled out as 'Then' indicates 'in that case'. We use 'then' with 'if' to talk about cause and effect but it cannot be used in association with 'no sooner' which is used in case of an event happening immediately after something else. 'After' shows "subsequently to the time when". Thus Option B can be discarded as it is clearly mentioned that two activities take place almost simultaneously.' For' explains reason or sights purpose. Thus Option C is discarded.

2. **(B)**

Correlative Conjunction is always used in pairs and denote equality, and show the relationship between ideas expressed in different parts of a sentence - and thus make the joining tighter and more emphatic. Some examples are either/or, neither/nor, and not only/but also. The structure no sooner is used to talk about something that happens immediately after something else. It is often used with the past perfect, and usually followed by than. In the given sentence it is inferred that the professor entered the classroom and immediately the students stood up. These two activities take place almost simultaneously. There is no real time difference between them. Thus Option B is correct. 'After' shows "subsequently to the time when". Thus Option D can be discarded as it is clearly mentioned that two activities take place almost simultaneously.' For' explains reason or sights purpose. Thus Option C is discarded. Option A can be ruled out as 'Then' indicates 'in that case'. We use 'then' with 'if' to talk about cause and effect but it cannot be used in association with 'no sooner' which is used in case of an event happening immediately after something else.

3. **(C)**

'So that' is used to talk about a purpose. In the given sentence, the purpose is to watch the stars. 'So that' is used to explain the purpose. Options A, B and D are grammatically wrong. Thus, option C is the correct answer.

4. **(A)**

'So that' is used to talk about a purpose. In the given sentence, the purpose is to get the work done. 'So that' is used to explain the purpose. Options B, C and D are grammatically wrong. Thus, option A is the correct answer.

5. **(D)**

'So that' is used to talk about a purpose. In the given sentence, the purpose is to not get dehydrated. 'So that' is used to explain the purpose. Options A, B and C are grammatically wrong. Thus, option D is the correct answer.

12. TENSES

Answer Key

1. Play	2. Does not write	3. Do not like	4. Did, Design	5. Towards
6. Did not crash	7. Took off	8. Will be	9. Will, help	10 Did not buy
11 Are not passing	12 Are, Trying	13 Is not walking	14. Was carrying	15. Were you not swimming
16. Were, yawning	17. Were swapping	18 Will be writing	19. Will be eating	20. Will be meeting

21. Has she been walking	22. Has been digging	23. Have not been cycling	24. Has not been reading	25. Had waiting been

HOTS (ACHIEVERS SECTION)

(A) 1. Megha eats cake	2. Megha ate cake	3. Megha was eating cake
(B) 1. I had read a book on Delhi's history	2. I was reading a book on Delhi's history	3. I have been reading a book on Delhi's history

13. JUMBLED WORDS

Answer Key

1. (B)	2. (C)	3. (A)	4. (C)	5. (C)	6. (B)	7. (A)	8. (C)	9. (B)	10. (C)
11. (B)	12. (B)	13. (C)	14. (C)	15. (D)	16. (B)	17. (C)	18. (D)	19. (C)	20. (A)

HOTS (ACHIEVERS SECTION)

21. (C)	22. (A)	23. (B)	24. (C)	25. (B)

14. VOICE AND NARRATION

Answer Key

1. (C)	2. (B)	3. (D)	4. (D)	5. (B)	6. (C)	7. (C)	8. (C)	9. (B)	10. (C)
11. (D)	12. (C)	13. (D)	14. (C)	15. (A)	16. (B)	17. (C)	18. (D)	19. (A)	20. (B)
21. (A)	22. (A)	23. (A)	24. (A)	25. (B)					

HOTS (ACHIEVERS SECTION)

26. (B)	27. (D)	28. (B)	29. (A)	30. (B)

26. (B) In this case, 'have caught and arrested" completes the sentence. It is an example of active voice.

29. (A) When the reporting verb is in past tense, the past continuous verb i.e. 'was coming' in the reported speech changes to past perfect continuous i.e. 'had been coming'. Thus the correct option is a.

30. (B) If the reporting verb (will say) is in the present or the future tense, the tense of the verb (did not like) in the reporting speech remains unchanged. Also, there wont be any change in the reporting verb (will say) But, 1st person pronoun (I) changes to 2nd person (he) in reported speech. So the final answer, combining the two rules, will be option (B).

Answer Key

1. His parents allowed him to celebrate the victory till late in the night.

2. He participated in the 1987 tournament in the capacity as a ball boy volunteer.

3. In 1992, he made his maiden appearance against England.

4. He described the 2007 World Cup as a forgettable since Indian team was eliminated quite early.

5. The importance of the 2011 World Cup lies in the fact that the speaker was a part of the World winning team.

1. Ronnie is narrating the story of Hachi – his grandfather's dog as a presentation on a topic on 'personal heroes'.

2. Professor Wilson decided to call the dog Hachiko because the word Hachi means good fortune in Japanese language.

3. Ken is a Japanese professor and colleague of Wilson.

4. The extraordinary behaviour of loyalty shown by Hachi towards his master by visiting the railway station where he worked and waiting for him every day for 10 years.

5. The sense of strong loyalty shown by Hachi is the focus of the profile published in the newspaper

1. Mangalyan was launched by ISRO from Sriharikota on November 5, 2013

2. National Space Agency (NSA) of the United States conferred the award named 'Space Pioneer Award.

3. (A) Became the first nation to place a spacecraft to orbit the planet Mars in the very first attempt.(B) The spacecraft takes high resolution images that are expected to help planetary scientists.

4. The award is a silvery pewter Moon globe cast by Baker Art Foundry from a sculpture originally created by well known space and astronomical scientist.

5. An ISRO official would receive the award during the 34th Annual Space Development Conference in Toronto, a large city in Canada.

Answer Key

1. (A)	2. (A)	3. (A)	4. (B)	5. (C)	6. (C)	7. (C)	8. (B)	9. (C)	10. (A)
11. (A)	12. (C)	13. (B)	14. (B)	15. (C)	16. (C)	17. (B)	18. (B)	19. (C)	20. (D)

HOTS (ACHIEVERS SECTION)

21. (A)	22. (B)	23. (A)	24. (A)	25. (D)

MODEL TEST PAPER

Answer Key

1. (D)	2. (A)	3. (C)	4. (B)	5. (A)	6. (A)	7. (B)	8. (C)	9. (A)	10. (B)
11. (A)	12. (C)	13. (B)	14. (A)	15. (C)	16. (C)	17. (B)	18. (D)	19. (A)	20. (C)
21. (B)	22. (B)	23. (D)	24. (A)	25. (C)	26. (D)	27. (A)	28. (C)	29. (C)	30. (C)
31. (A)	32. (C)	33. (C)	34. (B)	35. (C)					

SAMPLE OMR ANSWER SHEET

1. STUDENT NAME (IN ENGLISH CAPITAL LETTERS ONLY)

Students must write and darken the respective circles completely using HB Pencil only. Othewise their Answer Sheets will not be evaluated.

PERSONAL DETAILS

2. SCHOOL CODE

3. CLASS

4. SECTION

5. ROLL NO.

6. QUESTION PAPER SET

A ○ B ○ C ○ D ○

7. MOBILE NUMBER

8. GENDER

MALE ○

FEMALE ○

9. STREAM
(Only for Class XI and XII Students)

MATHEMATICS ○
BIOLOGY ○
OTHERS ○

MARK YOUR ANSWERS

1.	Ⓐ Ⓑ Ⓒ Ⓓ	26.	Ⓐ Ⓑ Ⓒ Ⓓ
2.	Ⓐ Ⓑ Ⓒ Ⓓ	27.	Ⓐ Ⓑ Ⓒ Ⓓ
3.	Ⓐ Ⓑ Ⓒ Ⓓ	28.	Ⓐ Ⓑ Ⓒ Ⓓ
4.	Ⓐ Ⓑ Ⓒ Ⓓ	29.	Ⓐ Ⓑ Ⓒ Ⓓ
5.	Ⓐ Ⓑ Ⓒ Ⓓ	30.	Ⓐ Ⓑ Ⓒ Ⓓ
6.	Ⓐ Ⓑ Ⓒ Ⓓ	31.	Ⓐ Ⓑ Ⓒ Ⓓ
7.	Ⓐ Ⓑ Ⓒ Ⓓ	32.	Ⓐ Ⓑ Ⓒ Ⓓ
8.	Ⓐ Ⓑ Ⓒ Ⓓ	33.	Ⓐ Ⓑ Ⓒ Ⓓ
9.	Ⓐ Ⓑ Ⓒ Ⓓ	34.	Ⓐ Ⓑ Ⓒ Ⓓ
10.	Ⓐ Ⓑ Ⓒ Ⓓ	35.	Ⓐ Ⓑ Ⓒ Ⓓ
11.	Ⓐ Ⓑ Ⓒ Ⓓ	36.	Ⓐ Ⓑ Ⓒ Ⓓ
12.	Ⓐ Ⓑ Ⓒ Ⓓ	37.	Ⓐ Ⓑ Ⓒ Ⓓ
13.	Ⓐ Ⓑ Ⓒ Ⓓ	38.	Ⓐ Ⓑ Ⓒ Ⓓ
14.	Ⓐ Ⓑ Ⓒ Ⓓ	39.	Ⓐ Ⓑ Ⓒ Ⓓ
15.	Ⓐ Ⓑ Ⓒ Ⓓ	40.	Ⓐ Ⓑ Ⓒ Ⓓ
16.	Ⓐ Ⓑ Ⓒ Ⓓ	41.	Ⓐ Ⓑ Ⓒ Ⓓ
17.	Ⓐ Ⓑ Ⓒ Ⓓ	42.	Ⓐ Ⓑ Ⓒ Ⓓ
18.	Ⓐ Ⓑ Ⓒ Ⓓ	43.	Ⓐ Ⓑ Ⓒ Ⓓ
19.	Ⓐ Ⓑ Ⓒ Ⓓ	44.	Ⓐ Ⓑ Ⓒ Ⓓ
20.	Ⓐ Ⓑ Ⓒ Ⓓ	45.	Ⓐ Ⓑ Ⓒ Ⓓ
21.	Ⓐ Ⓑ Ⓒ Ⓓ	46.	Ⓐ Ⓑ Ⓒ Ⓓ
22.	Ⓐ Ⓑ Ⓒ Ⓓ	47.	Ⓐ Ⓑ Ⓒ Ⓓ
23.	Ⓐ Ⓑ Ⓒ Ⓓ	48.	Ⓐ Ⓑ Ⓒ Ⓓ
24.	Ⓐ Ⓑ Ⓒ Ⓓ	49.	Ⓐ Ⓑ Ⓒ Ⓓ
25.	Ⓐ Ⓑ Ⓒ Ⓓ	50.	Ⓐ Ⓑ Ⓒ Ⓓ

Signature of the Student & Date of Examination

Signature of the Invigilator & Date of Examination

V&S Publishers, F-2/16 Ansari Road, Daryaganj, New Delhi-110002, ☎ 011-23240026-27
✉ info@vspublishers.com, 🌐 www.vspublishers.com

www.ingramcontent.com/pod-product-compliance
Lightning Source LLC
LaVergne TN
LVHW060356200726
843506LV00003B/237